THE SOFA SURFING HANDBOOK

WHEN I TOLD HIM HE COULD STAY ON OUR COUCH I MEANT IT, UM, RHETORICALLY, Y'KNOW?
TRY TELLING THAT TO HIM. HE THINKS HE'S BACK IN THE WOMB!
ZZZZZZ
POLITICS OF THE COUCH
OCCUPYING SOMEBODY ELSE'S COUCH REQUIRES CUNNING—BUT TO STAY INDEFINITELY ONE MUST ADHERE TO CERTAIN CRUCIAL UNWRITTEN LAWS......
BE OBSEQUIOUS, ACCEPT UNFAVORABLE BRANDS AND TEE-VEE SHOWS.
FOLDED BEDDING
ACCEPT LOCAL CUSTOMS AT FACE VALUE
OF COURSE WE DRY THE DISHES IN THE OVEN!
OTHERWISE WHERE WOULD THE CAT SLEEP?
BE INVISIBLE.
ZAP ZAP ZAP ZAP ZAP
TRY TO CONSOLIDATE THE AREA YOU'VE RENDERED USELESS TO THE TENANTS.
JAZZ FEST
EAT GLUTTONOUSLY ONLY IN THE DEAD OF NIGHT.
ZZZ
CLOSET
SLAM
WAIT UNTIL EVERYBODY GOES TO WORK BEFORE RIFLING THROUGH THEIR PERSONAL STUFF.

THE SOFA SURFING HANDBOOK

A GUIDE FOR MODERN NOMADS

JULIETTE TORREZ
EDITOR

MANIC D PRESS
SAN FRANCISCO

Dedicated to
everyone who ever let me stay on their couch
past, present, and future

EVER-LOVIN' DISCLAIMER: Just as almost everything in life is negotiable, so too everything is conditional and SUBJECT TO CHANGE without a moment's notice. A mention in this book does not imply endorsement. All opinions are those of the individual authors, and not necessarily those of the publisher or editor. All information is allegedly accurate as this goes to print but, hey, deal with it, okay? If you find something here that just ain't so, please be kind enough to let us know.

 For more information, write to Manic D Press, Box 410804, San Francisco, CA 94141 USA

Cover: Scott Idleman / BLINK. *Illustrations*: © Lloyd Dangle p. 2, 10; © Keith Knight p. 30, 37, 50, 54, 132; © Peter Bagge p. 78, 90, 106, 146, 154; © Jaime Hernandez p. 26, 43, 44, 58, 126, 131; © M. Kyle & Lisa Angelesco p. 120; © Eve Gilbert p. 158.

Library of Congress Cataloging-in-Publication Data

The sofa surfing handbook : a guide for modern nomads / Juliette Torrez, editor.

p. cm.
ISBN 0-916397-51-3
1. Travel--Guidebooks. I. Torrez, Juliette, 1966-
G153 .S654 1998
910'.2'02--ddc21

98-25459
CIP

Distributed to the trade by Publishers Group West

CONTENTS

POLITICS OF THE COUCH PART TWO
LONG BEFORE "COUCH POTATOS" BECAME TRENDY, THE COUCH HAS BEEN AN ESSENTIAL FURNISHING IN TROUBLETOWN. A HOTBED OF SLOTHFULNESS, NARCOLEPTIC IN ITS VERY DESIGN, THE COUCH MADE PROCRASTINATION POPULAR AND PUT THE AFTERNOON NAP ON THE MAP!
FLEAS
THE '39 DUST BOWL SURVIVOR
THE SWEAT-RESISTANT NAUGAHYDE THERAPY MODEL
"Sofa"
FIVE TON HIDE-A-BED
THE WEB O' SPRINGS DAVENPORT
THE FUTON (A POOR COUCH IMITATION)
VARIATIONS ON A THEME
A PARK BENCH
PARK BENCH WITH SCALLOP CUSHIONS (c. 1971) TERRIBLE!
A FUTON ON ITS OWN PARK BENCH
HISTORY BEARS THIS OUT.
WOW. I AM DEPRESSED.
ZZZZZ
DO NOT REMOVE THIS COMIC UNDER PENALTY OF LAW

FORWARD!

Some people are modern day gypsies, skipping from city to city without a budget, without a job, and sometimes even without the basic skills to ensure a roof over their heads. This is the thrill of the road, free as a bird, with few cares or responsibilities. It can also turn around and bite you in the ass if you aren't careful.

Breakups, evictions, unemployment, and poverty can put someone in the position to sofasurf. It can happen suddenly, without warning, and you're going to need to make decisions fast. Sometimes folks will sofasurf by choice as a way to save money, living rent free on a pal's couch for a while until they can get their proverbial shit together. I'll sofasurf for months at a time, using any money I earn for traveling.

Sofasurfing stints can vary from an overnighter to a months-long takeover of the living room. This book will show you how to set up a win-win situation for everyone involved. This can be a highly emotional time, as sofasurfing often occurs under stressful circumstances. The exception to this are the itinerant travelers; there is grace in knowing their stay will be finite. If you aren't a good houseguest, your benefactor will be clutching a steak knife before your stay is over.

This book doesn't assume that you have a credit card, but it does assume that you have debt and are not interested in incurring more. I don't need to sing to the choir about what the economy is like. The gap between rich and poor grows wider, there's a concentrated push for a plastic economy (ATM cards, check cards, credit cards) over cash and barter. Hotels are out of the travel budget, apartments are out of the survival budget. This book is not just for people who find themselves, whatever the circumstances, sofasurfing and only a few feet from homelessness but also for casual travelers with little money yet a great desire to explore the world. Survival tips for the road, how to arrive at your destination safely, and alternative modes of travel without the use of a credit card are found within.

Touring bands and travelers are adept at sofasurfing. It's an inexpensive way to visit other cities. If you're in a period of transition, this can be particularly comforting. Also, please remember that sofasurfing operates on the karmic wheel.

AM I A CAMPER?

This lifestyle isn't for everyone. Some people are to used to the amenities of clean sheets and fresh towels. That's nice, if you can get it and afford it. Sometimes you have to make do and be gracious about it. Bitchy and demanding people will have a hard time sofasurfing, since success is dependent on personal charm and respecting the sofa that you're surfing on.

The goal is to live as cheaply as possible during a period of transition, not to become a sponge off your friends and loved ones. If you overstay your welcome, you may be talking about some of these relationships in the past tense.

Along with being a sofasurfer, you'll also have to relinquish a little bit of personal power to your host. If your host gets passive-aggressive or abusive, recognize the behavior pattern and get out of the situation as quickly as possible without ruffling feathers. Sometimes, though, that can't be helped in an act of self-preservation. Los Angeles poet Iris Berry has this advice: "Be gracious and maintain your dignity." I think this is the social blueprint for successful sofasurfing.

Prepare to sleep in very strange places, some of them roach-infested, others the most beautiful places that time and money have created. Be grateful to everyone who has opened their doors to you, and try to be a good host to others when you have a place to live.

ESSENTIAL BELONGINGS LIST

underwear	2-3 tee shirts
1 pair of shorts	1 pair of leggings
2-3 pairs of pants or jeans	3-4 pairs of socks
1-2 long sleeved shirts	1 sweater or jacket
2 pairs of shoes	hat
towel	address book
driver's license or passport	personal items

Take clothes you can layer, especially when traveling in the winter months. Try to make sure they all match reasonably well. Include gloves and scarves, wool socks and an extra sweater or jacket. Black is all-purpose, and doesn't show stains but will act like a magnet for cat hair, so beware!

ESSENTIAL PERSONAL ITEMS

shampoo/conditioner	soap
toothbrush/toothpaste	brush/comb
deodorant	razor/shaving cream

lotion	tums/pepto-bismal tablets
aspirin/ibuprofen	bandaids/neosporin ointment
condoms	safety pins/rubber bands

FEM NOTE Pack a few pads and tampons, just in case. You never know when you'll need them, or run into someone who does. Traveling tends to knock your regular period off kilter, something to do with stress. Plus most facilities don't provide adequate supplies for such an emergency. And you can donate one to someone else in an emergency.

EXTRAS... Toiletries Bag

peppermint/rosemary oil	Tiger Balm
perfume	shower cap
nail polish/remover	cotton pads
nail clipper	barrettes/hair ties
foot lotion	cough drops

EXTRAS... Miscellaneous

vitamins	camera/film
pen and notebook	cassette recorder/walkman
extra cassettes	books
magazines	batteries
ear plugs	comic books
fetishes	universal sink stopper

computer diskette (loaded with your resume, writing, personal papers, addresses & phone numbers)

LUGGAGE

Make sure you have a good bag. Way too many bags fall apart in the waiting rooms of the Greyhound bus station, held together only by packing/duct tape. Get a good bag cheap at the local Goodwill. Try it there first. Check the zippers and the compartments. Make sure the handles are comfortable. Make sure it is approximately regulation size necessary for carry-on airplane travel. Another good place to shop for luggage is garage sales. Smell the bag to make sure the cat didn't do anything funny in it, and double check the stitching to make sure it won't fall apart during your first excursion. If , during your travels, your luggage does explode, reach for the duct tape (see below).

HAPPY CAMPER'S TIP

Tools of the Trade

There are two essential hardware items that can save your ass from oblivion when push comes to shove: duct tape and a Swiss Army knife. Now, it doesn't have to be an official Swiss Army knife, which can be expensive, but frankly some kind of pocket knife can be key. A basic Swiss Army knife has a can opener, a bottle opener, a mini scissors, a little blade and a bigger blade. Whether you're opening a bottle of beer that doesn't have a twist-off cap, opening a can of tuna, spreading peanut butter, or anything else that may require more than a fingernail, it's a super-nifty thing to have along just in case.

Kurt Zapata once wrote, "If you can't fix it with duct tape, that shit is broke." Jen once got her '71 VW camper up and running using duct tape alone. It's also useful for mending sneakers, sleeping bags, luggage, and just about everything else. No matter how you're traveling, invest a couple of bucks in a roll of duct tape. You'll sleep better at night knowing that you have it when things start falling apart.

THE BIG RULE

Take only as much as you can carry.

That's simple enough. Let me repeat, only take as much as you can carry comfortably. You're trying to pack light, right? Every time I break this rule, it invariably comes back and gives me a good kick in the teeth. If you have just finished packing and are unsure, then you've probably packed too much. Take this test: Load yourself down with all the stuff you're taking on this trip. Now walk with it to the end of the block. If you can't hack that, dump everything out and repack it half as much stuff.

I'm completely serious. Being coldhearted now will save you some pain down the line. Take it from experience. The less you take with you, the less you will have to worry about. Avoid taking items that will cause undue pain if lost or stolen. For your own peace of mind, take possessions that you own, not the things that own you.

The only time you can break the Big Rule is when you are confident and assured that you will have an extra set of hands helping you along the way, But rest assured, my sweet, the help won't come cheap. Remember that porters get tipped at least $1 per bag. If you have cabs in the budget, by all means, takes extra luggage. But if the cabbie doesn't help you with them, then decrease the standard tip, as he is obviously a dog.

HAPPY CAMPER'S TIP

All Purpose Soap

I like to refill my soap bottle at the local co-op with Dr. Bronner's almond or peppermint soap. This soap is good for brushing your teeth or washing your clothes if you're ever in a pinch. It tastes a little, umm, funky, but what's the difference? You're getting clean, aren't you? Regardless, always remember to carry your own soap. When it comes to sofasurfing, cleanliness is a key part of the ticket. Nobody wants a smelly pal stinking up the couch. And fer godsake don't leave a goddam mess in the bathroom. Mop up the post-shower water on the floor, wipe up the toothpaste drips or shaving dregs in the sink, straighten the towels, and most important, GUYS, put the damn toilet seat down if there's a female within 100 yards of the place. The toilet seat issue is a big one. Take my word for it. Don't ask, just deal with it. Really. Few behaviors create havoc more quickly than toilet seat etiquette.

DON'T DO THIS!

Stinky Feet

One time I was sofasurfing with this woman I hardly knew. She was really sweet, especially after I developed a terrible foot odor problem. She was horrified, but not nearly so much as me. The reasons partly had to do with my insistence on wearing black socks, but also because my diet was lacking zinc. So when you start to stink, take zinc and examine what you are eating. Also, foot powder (not talc!), white socks and peppermint foot lotion all do wonders for the alleviating this odoriferous predicament.

DECIDING WHAT TO WEAR

Stick to simple, partly because you don't want a hassle at the laundro and partly because you're trying to float through the scene with ease. Read the weather report for the region that you're visiting. Make room in the bag for a few accessories that will cheer you up when you're down. Ringling Sisters Iris Berry and Pleasant Gehman never travel without their tiaras and I don't know how many pairs of high-heeled shoes. Be prepared to roll with the punches, and don't forget you can always get whatever you forgot at the local Goodwill.

HAPPY CAMPER'S TIP

Gallon Plastic Bags

Undies, toiletries, and loose things fit nicely in gallon-sized resealable plastic bags. You can reuse the bags to hold dirty laundry and wet things. Don't forget to air out the wet things as soon as possible, otherwise mildew sets in and it really stinks and you have to rewash it anyway, usually using bleach.

WHILE AT THE LAUNDROMAT

With any laundromat, you get what you pay for. Laundromat washers are notorious for battering clothes full of holes and generally accelerating the wear and tear. If you have anything you cherish, handwash it in the sink.

(Handwash note: you can use your handy Dr. Bronner's soap and universal sink stopper. By the way, a universal sink stopper is a flat round piece of rubber which costs about $1 at grocery or drugstores. It's essential for handwashing clothes, dishes, hairbrushes, soaking tired feet, you name it.)

If the laundro advertises free dryers, expect to lug home an extra heavy basket of damp clothes because those damn dryers take forever to dry a load of clothes containing anything heavier than socks and underwear. Washers generally run about $1.25 per load.

Some of these places offer laundry service, wash and fold for 50 cents a pound. If you are truly lazy or like to spoil yourself, this is another option. Avoid dry cleaning. It's just too expensive, and clothes like that have no business being with you on this trip.

Of course, the best method is to use a friend's washer and dryer, but remember to bring your own laundry detergent or give them a buck towards the amount of theirs you used.

HAPPY CAMPER'S TIP

Sewing Kit

Save some money and don't plan on buying clothes while you're on the road. Invest in a standard mending kit, and repair your clothes on a regular basis. Repair those buttons while they're still hanging by a thread - once they're gone, they're gone. You'll be surprised at how quickly your clothes will develop holes while you're traveling. In an emergency, safety pins'll keep it together, and in a pinch I've used masking tape to hold up hems and cuffs. Just take the tape off before putting the clothes in the washer.

DON'T DO THIS!

The Broken Shoe

Whatever you do, do not persist in taking anything that needs to be fixed. There is little room in your luggage as it is, certainly not enough room for something like a broken shoe. If you must, go buy or borrow some Krazy Glue and see what you can do to fix the shoe. After you've given up (and I guarantee, you will give up), leave the shoe and its mate. Shoes are replaceable, that's part of the beauty of shoes, shopping for new ones. In a pinch, for gals during the summer, I recommend the traditional Chinese babydoll slippers (unless you're doing a lot of walking, then you'll need something sturdier). They are cheap and plentiful, available at any Walmart or import shop, and take no room in your luggage.

Limit yourself to three pairs of shoes when you travel: walking shoes, evening shoes, and sneakers.

For something more dressy, most urban centers have really great shoe stores. My favorite place to go show shopping? El Paso/Juarez. You can find some great leather products in the latter, but I suspect it's because one of the world's largest cattle bins is located outside the city limits. The most trendy? New York City. The goods are cheap and flashy but that's the way I like it sometimes.

ABOUT THAT TEESHIRT

Always be aware of your environment. When you live too long on either of the coasts, it's really easy to think that the rest of the country shares your view. I mean, we all get the same MTV, right? Not quite. Remember that all the freaks flock to the cities because that's what you do when you're a little 'different' and growing up in small town Americana: you dream of going someplace else.

A word of warning when traveling through Middle America, which exists about 30 miles outside of every major metropolitan center: don't bring any unwanted attention to yourself by wearing marijuana leaves, obscenities, and/or drug references. Law enforcement agencies, those sworn to protect and to serve, are just looking for a probable cause to search and seize your possessions on drug traffic allegations. Don't think it happens? Let me give you a healthy dose of paranoia. I don't know about you, but I don't have the time or money for costly legal fees or court costs, so I avoid the issue entirely by wearing nondescript clothing.

I'm not saying to edit yourself or censor your tee shirts, but don't be stupid. When traveling in unfamiliar territory you might want to check out the climate before you start heating things up for yourself. The point is to get through your travels with ease, not conflict. Unless, of course, you enjoy conflict. Sometimes I do. Sometimes, I know it's asking for trouble.

Many small towns and counties throughout the U.S. pay the local cops' salaries with fines paid by people they pick up for minor infractions (driving over the speed limit, running a stop light, etc.). Drug laws vary from state to state, and having one pot seed in your car or suitcase is a felony in some states. Be aware! They *are* out to get you! If confronted by a cop, be polite and very respectful. Answer questions with a simple 'Yes, sir' or 'No, sir', even if the cop appears to be twelve years old. Tell them you are on your way to visit your very old Aunt Bessy in the next town and she's expecting you for dinner. Tell them there's been a death in the family. Try to avoid cops if at all possible! Always! Remember, cops are here to hassle you.

DON'T DO THIS!

Exploding Luggage

Sometimes when you've been on the road, your luggage will want to explode and does, right in the middle of a friend's living room. I am always grateful for the opportunity to unleash my baggage, but I know in my heart that I am being a Bad Camper. Do your unpacking in a discreet corner of the house, rather than in the front room. Everyone will be a lot happier and the living room will stop looking like someone's bedroom. Don't forget to pack up your bedding every morning when you get up, otherwise the living room will look a little too lived in.

DON'T DO THIS!

Traveling with Animals

A couple was traveling through the country, performing in coffeehouses and car camping along the way. They had their dog with them, and stayed at a friend's house one night. The family had a menagerie of pets, including a hutch of rabbits penned in the backyard.

During the night, the couple's dog broke into the pen and tore the bunnies apart. Surprisingly enough, the family took it well. The youngest parlayed the tragedy as an opportunity to lobby for a cat. But still, it's a terrible thing to be remembered as the houseguest who killed the family pets.

I never travel with animals. You are totally responsible for another life and the actions of that life. It's really upsetting to see street kids panhandling for their pets' food. If you can't take care of your pet, you have no business owning one.

PAMPER YOURSELF

When things get really stressful, take a break and treat yourself. Find the nearest public library and read a book or magazine. Go perusing the cut-out bins at the record store, or the under-a-dollar box at the used book store. Hit the local happy hour places that offer free food. Splurge on a bargain movie matinee.

Gals, treat yourself to a $6 manicure, or go deluxe and get a new 'do. Salons are always looking for haircut models, and for $10 or less, you can get a raging new hairstyle. Salons looking for models usually advertise on the back page of the free local alternative newspaper, or try calling around and asking. Since the salon'll be practicing a certain style (e.g., bobs), you can't be too choosy, and this is definitely *not* the way to go if you only want a trim.

©Jaime Hernandez

HELPFUL HINTS FOR SOFA SURFING WITH HIV

JUSTIN CHIN

Traveling with a 24/7 condition like HIV can add special challenges to an already unusual reality. Here are a few ideas to ensure a safe, fun, and hassle-free adventure.

WATCH OUT for other people's cats. Just 'cause you keep your cat box winterfresh clean and get your kitty-cat her shots, doesn't mean that everyone else does too. Cat poop can transmit toxoplasmosis, which is some evil kind of amoeba-bacteria-parasite thing that eats your brain in your skull! (Not exactly the correct medical terms for what ensues, but essentially, that's what happens.) Not a pleasant thing by any means. Interestingly, dog shit doesn't have that parasite, so I'm told, so go ahead and lick that poodle's poop off the pavement.

REMEMBER your medications. People with HIV can take up to 20/30-odd pills a day. I like to get a good airtight container and dump them all in. Airtight is a good idea because moisture can really fuck up those pills.

IF you run out of pills, or get moisture in them, or leave them at a trick's house along with half your possessions and can't get to them because he/she's turned psycho, you can get your physician to call your prescriptions in to almost any pharmacy in the country. Walgreen's, Thrifty's, Rite-Aid, Stadlanders, and all those good chains are easy to find. Check your medical insurance/Medicaid and know which chain pharmacies will accept your health coverage. Not all pharmacies can fill the prescription in a day, some may take a few days to have the medications sent in, so be prepared. Have your necessary insurance cards with you, your doctor's numbers, and all that information. You should have it chucked in your wallet or handbag, anyway.

Your immune system is not as up to snuff as it used to be. For god's sake, spend a few pennies and buy bottled water. (Check to see that the seal is not broken and the grocery store has filled it with tap water. Hey, I'm from the Third World, I'm cautious.)

RELAX and take it easy. Don't stress yourself out unnecessarily. Eat well and eat often. Party, drink and screw around in moderation and according to what your body can handle. Sing Hakuna Matata to yourself quietly or in a karaoke bar.

IF you're travelling abroad, you might face some problems if customs finds all these HIV drugs in your possession. Often, they can deny you entry into the country. The U.S. can deny non-citizens entry based on that. I'm not saying that you should declare them. I'm also not saying that you should put them in a different bottle labelled Multivitamins or Aspirin. I'm also not saying that you should pack about a few days' worth and Fed-Ex or mail the rest to someone in the country you're going to. Just saying that you should know that this might happen.

ONE of the ickiest side effects of HIV drugs and HIV disease is the diarrhea. It's not pleasant and I don't know anyone who hasn't had at least one unfortunate accident. Remember to carry a small pack of tissues with you and if you can, bring extra underwear. If it's really bad, adult diapers are really not a bad idea especially if you're on a long Greyhound ride.

REMEMBER, even in this day and age, there are still a lot of people who are ignorant, prejudiced and fearful of people with HIV. They may freak out when you tell them, kick you out of their houses, or try to kill you. Be careful of whom and how you reveal your HIV status.

Man.. I just gotta Thank you fer lettin' me STAY here This long... I'll be outta here as soon as possible.. And about the phone bill...I thought 1-900 numbers were FREE!!
©Keith Knight

SUGARING YOUR VISIT

Leaving gifts for your hosts is one of the nicest ways to say thank you.

groceries	flowers
wine	herbal tea
beer	coffee
comics or magazines	water pipe

For style points, bake something for the household. The full-blown sensory experience of walking into a place that smells like homemade brownies, cookies, or muffins fresh from the oven rules, and is a great (and cheap) way to convey one's gratitude. Whether you pick up a box of Duncan Hines brownie mix (throw in some chocolate chips and/or raisins for extra fun), or bake one of the following recipes from scratch, this is a tried-and-true technique for securing future invitations.

Remember to check with your host before turning on the oven. If it hasn't been cleaned or used for a long time, and/or there are definitely roaches in the kitchen, you should avoid baking in it. Roaches enjoy the darkness and warmth provided by an old stove that's never used, so when you turn it on a scene from a Stephen King novel will ensue as all of the critters bail out onto the floor and counters. Ugh! Make pancakes on Sunday instead.

All of the ingredients in the following recipes are readily available, just remember to get a disposable aluminum muffin tin or cookie sheet if necessary. Hell, buy a cheap real one at a thrift store, and give it to the house with a copy of the recipe.

Yummy Pancakes

1 1/2 cups flour
2 1/2 teaspoons baking powder
1/4 teaspoon salt
1 egg
1 1/4 cup milk
2 tablespoons melted butter or oil

Sift together flour, baking powder, and salt. Mix milk, egg, and oil thoroughly. Add milk mixture to dry ingredients, and stir lightly. Do not overmix - batter should be hella lumpy! Add sliced bananas or blueberries to batter. Drop by the spoonful onto hot, greased skillet. Serve with syrup, honey, yogurt, or jam. Yay!

Amazing Oatmeal Raisin Chocolate Chip Cookies

1/2 cup butter
3/4 cup brown sugar
1 egg
3/4 teaspoon vanilla
3/4 cup flour
1/2 teaspoon baking soda
1/4 teaspoon salt
1/2 teaspoon cinnamon
1/4 teaspoon nutmeg
1 1/2 tablespoons milk
1 1/2 cups oats
chocolate chips
raisins

Preheat oven to 350 degrees. Cream together butter, brown sugar, egg, and vanilla. Sift in flour, baking soda, salt, cinnamon, and nutmeg. Mix in milk and oats until blended. Add chocolate chips and raisins. Drop by the spoonful onto greased baking pan. Bake for 10 minutes or until done. Remember, every oven heats and bakes differently, so use caution and check those cookies often.

Banana Blueberry Muffins Supreme

2 cups flour
3 tablespoons sugar
2 1/2 teaspoons baking powder
1/2 teaspoon salt
1/2 teaspoon cinnamon
1 egg
1 cup milk
2 tablespoons canola oil
2 mashed very ripe bananas
frozen or fresh blueberries

Preheat the oven to 400 degrees. Sift together the flour, sugar, baking powder, and salt. Beat the egg with the milk and oil, and mix well with the banana mush. Add the wet ingredients to the dry, stirring only until no flour shows. It should lumpy - whatever you do, do not overmix. Gently add blueberries and spoon into greased muffin tin. Bake approximately 25 minutes.

Don't forget to make the kitchen spotless when you're done baking. I mean, what's the point of baking something delicious if you leave a sink full of dishes?

COMIC BOOK READING LIST

Everyone loves comic books. At least, all the folks I know. I'll buy a batch of alternative comic books at the beginning of any trip, that way I always have something to read and at the same time, something to leave at friends' houses when I visit.
Highly recommended titles:

Hate
Milk & Cheese
Troubletown
Weirdo
New Love
Love & Rockets
Dirty Plotte
Slutburger
Zap
Whoa Nellie

MAGAZINE READING LIST

The same goes for magazines, which can be a luxury for many folks, as some publications run about an hour's wage:

Flipside
Juxtapoz
Bust
Grand Royal
High Times
Gearhead

One of my friends who had a couple crashing in her living room for a substantial length of time was thrilled when they got her a six-month subscription to the Sunday *New York Times* on their departure. It was something she truly coveted, and she thought nice things about her houseguests every Sunday for six months after their departure. Those pals will always be welcome in the future. What a concept! That reasonably-priced, thoughtful gift was a helluva lot cheaper than two weeks in a San Francisco hotel.

HOW LONG IS TOO LONG?

The best rule of thumb is gypsy law, which is six days, according to NYC poet Hal Sirowitz. There are houses that are sofasurfing savvy and it may be possible to extend your stay for weeks in a calm, peaceful and productive environment. Don't assume everyone in the living situation shares the same sentiment, and don't forget to thank the housemates with a follow-up note or postcard.

KNOW WHEN TO GO

No matter who you are, whether you're an amateur or pro, it's essential to know when to go. Overstaying one's welcome will guarantee no future couch reservations, may terminate a friendship forever, and generally earn you an unwanted reputation as a social pariah and, well... bum.

LEAVE IMMEDIATELY WHEN

• your host is fighting in the next room with his/her significant other
• you get cornered in the shower by a roommate
• there are junkie strangers in the kitchen at 2 a.m. looking for clean needles
• people are already sleeping on the living room floor
• you become the subject of the fights

Rent?.. Oh yeah... I don't know what happened... My dad was sup-posed to send a check...
Is it okay if my friend Citrus stays here? Just until she comes down...
Eh.. what the heck.. it's only three weeks late, right?
five months at the most.

WHEN FRIENDS COME TO STAY... AND STAY... AND STAY

JENNIFER JOSEPH

As the giant wheel of karma turns, paybacks are a bitch. The more sofasurfing you do, the more people will come and crash at your place, if and when you ever settle down.

Prior to living happily ever after in San Francisco, I drove across America six times in four years taking a different route each time, staying with friends, acquaintances, relatives, friends of friends, friends of friends of friends, relatives of friends, et al. When word got out that I had my name on a lease, the deluge of visitors began. It was not unusual for both couches and rugs to be full of crashed-out houseguests, particularly in the week between Christmas and New Year's.

HASTA LA VISTA, BABY

To get an unwelcome houseguest off the couch, first hint about when he or she is leaving - "So, where are you off to next?" When the reply is noncommittal - "Not really sure, still thinking about it," do not hesitate to be direct. Give him or her a day of departure - "It's been great having you here, really, but you need to be out of here by Tuesday because..." (pick one) a. my mother is coming to visit; b. my roommates are freaking out; c. someone else is showing up who made prior couch reservations; d. I desperately need my space back.

If nothing else works, buy a box of large Hefty trash bags, pack their shit up for them, and put the bags next to the door. Wait by the door. When you hear the key in the lock, grab the door and open it quickly, grab their key before they have a chance to react (the element of surprise is important here). Announce "That's it. I hope you don't mind but I took the liberty of helping you pack. Here's your stuff. Take it easy." Hopefully, they're still outside the door and you can heft their Hefty trash bags at them, remove the key from the lock, and shut the door in one fell swoop. Do this very quickly, and then pour yourself a stiff drink, fill a bong hit, or go watch *Jeopardy* or something. Remember to do this only as a last resort because it's way gnarly and no fun whatsoever. Nightmare. I've actually had to do this, but only once, thank god.

If your unwelcome houseguest has a key to your place, you may need to think about changing the locks, a small expense compared to having all of your stuff ripped off somewhere down the line. Too many housekeys floating around is never a good idea. Get a forwarding number or address for that person, who will inevitably get calls or people trying to locate them in the future.

IF YOU'RE HOSTING...

• Find out immediately who the guy on the couch is and how he's connected to the roommates. Once upon a time in a big group-house in Berkeley... For three days everyone in the house assumed the guy on the couch was someone else's pal until David spoke up and said he was just some hitchhiker he had picked up on the drive down from Eugene. He didn't even know the guy's name. Yikes! The guy'd been on the sofa for three days. We made Dave tell him it was time to hit the road

• Generosity has its limits. We were crashing at Len and Frank's parents' place in Pittsburgh, PA on the way across country and had picked up a hitchhiker who seemed slightly scruffy but nonetheless civilized. Arriving late at night in P-burg, Len said it was okay for the hitchhiker to crash at the house too. In the morning, hitchhiking-guy couldn't find the bathroom so he took a leak outside on Mrs. S.'s prized rose bushes. Unfortunately, Mrs. S was looking out the window at the time, and what ensued is not worth repeating. Needless to say, we made a hasty exit and left Nature-Boy at the highway on-ramp.

• Generosity has its limits, take two. One day, when Chris was staying at Jon's flat located near the infamous corner of Haight and Ashbury, he was the only one there. A totally gross street bum rang the doorbell and said, "Hey, man, someone said it'd be cool to take a shower here." So Chris let him in. Meanwhile, Jim came home and was like, "Who's in the shower?" Chris told him about the guy ringing the doorbell and all, and of course Jim freaked out. Lesson learned: always tell your guests the house rules, whether it's no smoking cigarettes in the house, no letting in strangers, whatever. Even if it seems like common sense to you, some people have no sense. At all.

• Think globally, act locally: Jay-who-was-in-jail-in-Jersey was a wheatgrass-chomping, brewer's-yeast-sprinkling, remarkably effusive pal who had plenty of global consciousness but displayed very little when it came to other people asleep in the flat. One morning after a lo-o-o-o-o-ng night of massive partying, the eight people crashed out in various rooms throughout the apartment were jarringly awakened by the sound of undercooked garbanzo beans in a blender at high-speed. To my drug-addled mind the sound was somewhere between a '66 Volkswagen with transmission trouble and machine gun flak. When I stumbled into the kitchen and asked, "What the fuck are you doing?" Jay replied "Making hummus." At 10 a.m. in a house full of sleeping people, whatever you do, don't ever EVER do that.

• When "thank you" and an imported six-pack will suffice: Frank from Frankfurt was this pal of Jeffree' s. He was from Germany and went to massage school in

Humboldt County with Jeffree and needed a place to crash in San Francisco while he took care of some visa stuff to stay in the country. So fine, he had a few night's reservations on the sofa. On the last night of his visit, Frank offered to give David a massage since David's back was kind of tweaked. Since Frank went to massage school and all, David thought it was a splendid idea. Truthfully, a decent backrub would have sufficed, but evidently Frank triggered a few acupressure points that caused David to become violently ill the next day, after Frank had left, of course. Beware! Stick to six-packs and pints of ice cream!

WHAT KIND OF FRIEND WON'T EVEN LET YOU BORROW THEIR COUCH FOR ONE LOUSY, STINKIN' NIGHT?
SHIT--- FUCK--- PISS---

©Jaime Hernandez

HOUSESITTING HEAVEN

Usually, if you're housesitting, you are responsible for no more than taking in the mail, watering the plants and feeding the animals. If you clean up after yourself, there should be no problem. Try to make extra time to leave the house cleaner than when you arrived. If you don't clean up, you'll be sure to hear about it from the homeowner and maybe even lose your housesitting privileges. If the hosts say to help yourself to whatever's in the fridge, go on ahead, but try to leave something for the hosts when they return, schedule and finances permitting.

CHORES ANYONE CAN DO
(meaning you)

- Wash the car
- Fill the gas tank
- Feed the animals
- Wash the dishes

Vacuum	Put air in the bike tires
Water the garden	Clean the bathroom
Wash the linens	Wash the floor

HOUSESITTER'S TIP

Stocking the Fridge

Include the staples of any American refrigerator. If your benefactors are returning from a trip, the last thing they will want to do is go to the grocery store.

Eggs	Bread
Milk	Cheese
Beer	Chips/cookies
Juice	Fruit
Coffee	Bagels

PAYING FOR LONG DISTANCE

Do not make long-distance calls from someone else's phone. Don't do it. At all. Instead, buy a pre-paid phone card. This way you'll avoid incurring debt, wrath, and annoyance. Just because someone's letting you crash at their house doesn't mean they're made out of money.

DON'T DO THIS!

Getting Locked Out of the House

This is the worst. Try to anticipate this moment but making a spare key ahead of time and burying it in the backyard or under a flower pot somewhere. Sometimes the owners will give an extra key to a neighbor for just such an emergency - remember to ask about it ahead of time. If not, you're going to have pay exorbitant amounts for a locksmith to come and let you in. And you better be sure that those keys are indeed inside the house, because it will cost you extra for the locksmith to make keys for you. Avoid having this happen on weekends, because the housecall rate doubles.

Some people have actually broken into the house in which they were housesitting, but it makes for a terrible situation when the shattered panes of glass are lying at your feet and you're trying to explain to the horrified neighbors that you are the housesitter.

HOUSESITTER'S TIP
Meeting the Neighbors

Make it a point to go around in the first few days of your stay and introduce yourself to the neighbors. That way they will know your face and not eye you so suspiciously when they walk past in the morning. Also, these folks can help if you run into any trouble. If you bake, even better: bring them some cookies.

THROWING PARTIES

General rule, don't do it. If there is damage, your hosts are sure to find out about it, and believe you me, they will not be pleased. Limit yourself to one dinner guest at a time, and make sure your guest observes the house rules, whether it's no smoking inside, no shoes on the white rug, whatever.

BEING NOSY

Again, the general rule of thumb is, don't do it. Peruse the bookshelves and the bric-a-brac but don't let your explorations go any farther. People don't appreciate having their belongings rifled. Plus, we all have our nasty little secrets. Are you sure you want to know theirs? Yuck.

WATERING THE PLANTS

If not previously specified by the owners, most plants only need water once or twice a week. Feel the dirt an inch down in the pot. If it's dry, the plant needs water. Don't overwater — the plant should not be sitting in a giant swimming pool at the bottom. Overwatering kills plants more often than not watering at all! If plants begin to droop that's another sure sign to give them a drink. Let the soil dry out between waterings to avoid root rot. Trim off dead leaves and spent flowers to keep plants healthy-looking.

TAKING CARE OF PETS

Make sure you have an affinity with the animals. Once I was taking care of a cockatiel that belonged to friends, when the bird decided to make a break for it out the back door. I caught up with it at the chainlink fence, where he was poised to make a leap over the ivy. When I grabbed him with both hands, he turned around and bit me good. It could have been worse, he could have bitten my fingers off, but fortunately he was just voicing his displeasure and I got off lucky with small wounds, and massive heart palpitations over losing my friend's pet while they were gone.

Another friend of mine was caring for a pet snake. A huge pet snake. It got sick and the vet put the snake on antibiotics. It took four people to hold the snake down, and they had to find a junkie off the street to administer the medication.

Miles Long related a story about a friend, Paul, who was housesitting and had never met the cat before his housesitting stint. Fluffy was an indoor-outdoor cat who happened to be outside when the owners left. After a few days, Paul wondered why Fluffy wasn't around but was horrified that the neighbor's cat kept trying to come in the cat door. Naturally, Paul kept shooing him out. Needless to say, when the owners came back, Paul learned that the neighbor's cat he wouldn't let in was, of course, Fluffy. Yikes! Meet the animals in advance.

©Keith Knight

OTHER PEOPLE'S CATS

ANGELA MOSKOW

A seasoned couch surfer is wise to cultivate skills which may prove useful to a host or hostess. Cat sitting is one such skill. It has the added advantage of often resulting in an upgrade from a couch to the most comfortable bed in the house when the host departs. Of course, this may be in exchange for a few scratches if the cat would prefer to spend the time outside of your company.

I've lived an hour-and-a-half away from San Francisco for the past three years, and have gotten to know quite a few of my friends' cats during this time. I grew up with cats, but don't have any of my own now. I generally enjoy the time spent getting to know these felines. Make cat sitting as pleasant as possible for everyone involved by asking a few questions and learning to deal with the small disturbances that will inevitably occur.

Observing a cat with a furball for the first time is an alarming experience. The unique sound of a retching cat is striking, and could inspire the uninitiated to perform the Heimlich maneuver on poor Inky. Unfortunately, furballs inhabit cat territory. While most seem to come up in the middle of the night, they may also be left as presents to greet you at the end of a long day. Other gifts from kitties include birds (sometimes in embryonic form), mice, and other critters. During mating season, expect a sprayed doorway, or if it's a feral cat, spraying may be an everyday event.

Lookout for the almighty flea, a problem on cats who stray out of doors. Indoor cats will try to convince you that they patrol their neighborhoods. Outdoor cats take liberties when their owner is away, and may not appear for days to protest the new living arrangement. Inquire about the cat's propensity to wander, that way you'll know when to file a missing kitty report.

Try to stick to the cat's eating, litter box, and exercise routines since they lend some semblance of normality to what are otherwise disrupted times. Remember that the cat is the permanent member of the household, and that you are the outsider. Strange habits abound. I've been woken up by a cat playing with my hair, and another grand old cat spent most of the time sleeping in the baby's bassinet.

Every cat has a different dietary regime. Don't try to remember a cat's diet, instead ask for written instructions specifying the menu and the timing. Some cats do perfectly well with dry food every few days, while others require more constant culinary attention.

I once heard of a cat named Krakatoa who ate tuna and steamed broccoli mixed with his medication. The most gastronomically advanced cat that I know eats four small meals each day, and an occasional potato when he's been good. All of the cats I've met drink tap water, although some prefer water from toilets. This, of course, requires regular flushing by humans.

Familiarize yourself with litter box requirements. While perhaps not as varied as diets, kitty bathroom rituals span the spectrum from the latest in kitty litter technology to great outdoors as catbox. I even know a cat that uses the toilet rather than a litter box, and he never falls into the bowl. Most cats don't require much attention outside of the realms of food and catbox, but one cat has a morning exercises/play routine. This is the same cat that plays with my hair while I'm sleeping, so he's likely the Arnold Schwarzenegger of cats.

Get the information on the cat's veterinarian. I have not yet had a kitty health emergency. If my friends are relaxing on a beach they'd rather not get a call if their feline friend has been in a fight and needs stitches.

Last, and most important, is purchase a cheap little water pistol. Despite one's best intentions, a cat scratch is a badge of honor. You can always fight back with a water pistol. After stumbling to the bathroom in the middle of the night, I returned to a bedroom doorway blocked by a hissing cat in attack mode. A glass of water in his face allowed me safe passage. I subsequently roamed the halls armed with a water pistol at all times. Water is a cat's worst enemy, and Scooter mellowed out considerably after getting squirted in the chops a few times. Walk softly, but carry a loaded water pistol.

YOU NEVER REALIZE HOW MUCH STUFF YOU'VE ACCUMULATED UNTIL THE DAY YOU MOVE OUT..
But it's an urn..., with you father's ashes in it!!
Five bucks and it's yours.
IT GETS TO THE POINT WHERE YOU'LL GET RID OF ANYTHING JUST TO LIGHTEN UP THE LOAD..

DOMESTIC MOMENTS

PHIL WEST

As a happily married person with a solid job living in a great house loaded with wedding gifts and Ikea furniture, the last thing I expected to be doing in the summer of '97 was bouncing between households, portaging a sliver of my belongings from place to place. But when my wife fell in love with one of my friends and effectively flipped the off-switch on our seven-year relationship, the only option was pretty clear. I had to get out of the house rather than continue to watch her grow this new love into her flower and my weed.

The pragmatic thing to do would have been find a new place right away. But materialism won out. I wanted a new computer printer. I wanted pots and pans. I wanted to nest. And to do it right, to save the necessary bucks for a deposit on a new place and a cornucopia of new gadgets, I knew I would have to take to the couches of my friends: Mike with his comfortable, lived-in duplex; Jennifer with her treehouse apartment; and my favorite professors, Phil and Sabrina, who gave me the cherriest of cherry housesitting assignments in the middle of all of this. So how does the domestically-inclined guy do it right? Here's my guide to successful couchsurfing for the terminal nester:

Voice Mail

Lost messages? Being tied to the phone in your temporary domicile? Having nothing to do at work with an idle phone at your side with no supervision? Voice mail eradicates those problems, and if you attach it to a pager, as I did, it becomes a lifeline to the outside world. $10 a month is a small price to pay for the peace of mind it brings.

The Fine Folks at Public Storage

With a first-month fee of only one dollar and a security system which seems to run with Orwellian efficiency, it's hard not to recommend Public Storage. Once you get over the displacement of putting most of your life in a 5 x 10 closet, it's easy to travel light knowing that your non-essentials are being treated with reverence. For one of my friends, essentials meant clothes and a honeybear full of Dr. Bronner's peppermint soap in a ridiculous black bag made by fitting leather over a couple of hubcaps. For me, this meant two crates full of clothes, a backpack, and a bag full of personal papers, which all fit inside the trunk of my car. The car, admittedly, is a luxury that many of my couchsurfing friends don't have, but then again, most of my couchsurfing friends started from a place less stable.

Cable TV

The equalizer. The conversation piece. The blessed source of escape and distraction. There's a Burl Ives song that goes, "When in life, make this your goal: watch the donut, not the hole." And cable TV is the ultimate donut. If my friend Mike and I were lovers, the ESPN theme music would be our song. Remember, you are the guest. Under no circumstances are you to dominate the clicker. Hand it over without hesitation the moment a rent-paying resident walks in the room. Do not make negative comments about their choice of programming, be it the home shopping channel or reruns of *Cheers*.

Move Around

This wasn't my intention, but it's good to do if you can do it because you never wear out your welcome. There's also an etiquette you fall into. You will get into late-night conversations which go later than you might expect. Roll with it. You'll learn more about your friends and yourself. Surprise them. Do their dishes. Recycle their beer bottles. Throw away their stale half-eaten bags of tortilla chips. Even if you never put on the French maid's outfit and trigger some unknown fetish lurking inside your host, you will be an endearing part of his or her life rather than someone sucking energy and domesticity out of the room. And then you'll go before the imprint of your body subtly changes the landscape of the couch you're sleeping on. I did. And it sure beat paying rent.

ROADTRIPPING

Nothing compares to driving down the highway. I love the feeling of constant motion. A road trip can be a lifelong bonding experience between friends or strangers, where destination and a good time are shared goals. When traveling with two or three other people, roadside motels suddenly become affordable. Concerts, festivals, Disneyland, the Indy 500, Mardi Gras, these are all some excellent reasons to pack up the car and go go go.

COMMON SENSE ROAD TIPS

- Take some money.
- If you can't take money, take something of value that you can trade or pawn.
- Be willing to work.
- Let a friend or two know your itinerary, so that

someone worries if you come up missing.

- Take appropriate identification.
- Avoid the states with outstanding warrants.

RULES OF THE ROAD

- Stop for accidents if no one else has already, you might be the only calm, sane person with bandages.
- Don't hassle truckers.
- Don't flip off other motorists, especially on long stretch of backwater roads. Haven't you ever seen *Easy Rider*?

ROAD TIP

Stocking Your Car

Make sure the care is stocked with the following:

Blanket	First aid kit
Gallon of water	Fix-a-flat
Quart of oil	Duct tape
Fire extinguisher	Thermos
Flashlight	Road flares
Spare tire and jack	

STOPPING FOR STRANDED MOTORISTS

It's good karma to stop if elderly people and women are broken down by the side of the road. Assess a situation and trust your intuition if it seems safe. Don't be a do-gooder and endanger yourself. Women travelers should not stop for men who are broken down. If you don't want to stop, make a note of the mile marker and call the local highway department.

You never might know when you'll be the first person on an accident scene. One night I was driving down Interstate 5 somewhere in Oregon when I suddenly came upon a car that had just overturned in the rain. I pulled over, put my blinkers on, got my emergency flares and placed them behind the car so no one would collide into it. Another motorist had a cell phone, so within moments there was a team of handsome firemen at the accident scene patching up the driver (who was unhurt, lucky for him).

ROAD TIP

AAA

Memberships at the American Automobile Association run about $45/year. Membership ensures a free tow from wherever you break down to a nearby fix-it shop. AAA will also open your car for free if you lock your keys inside, jumpstart a dead battery, and bring you a gallon of gas in an emergency. Even if an AAA member is a passenger in the car, not the driver, these offers are still good. Plus, they have offices all over the country and will heap free maps on you for the asking. AAA will also, in a pinch, cash a member's check up to $50. American Express traveler's checks are available to members without a service charge at any AAA office. If you're driving anywhere, it's a pretty good investment.

AUTO CHECKLIST

Before you drive any distance, check the following:

tire pressure	oil level
water level	belts and hoses

If you aren't careful, one of these easy maintenance things may leave you stranded at the side of the road and you'll find you and your girlfriend pushing the car at a jog down some Arizona highway at night when what you really wanted was Mexican beaches. Fill the gas tank before you hit the highway. When it's the only gas station around for miles, they can charge whatever they want, and they do.

ROAD TIP

Lube Shops

If you have your car regularly serviced at a national chain lube shop, they will often top it off for you for free between the 3,000-mile visits.

SPLITTING THE HOTEL COSTS

When there are three or more people traveling together, sharing a hotel or motel room for the evening is recommended. Don't try to sneak in on a single room; pay for a double and avoid any potential hassles.

Before you pay for one of these late night roadside lodgings, ask to see the room. Make sure it's clean, that the shower and toilet run properly, that there are no bugs in the bed and that the sheets and towels are clean.

Also, if you arrive in town late at night, you can

sometimes get a deal on a room. These folks just want to rent a room, and it's better to have a room rented than not. So don't hesitate to ask for a possible discounted rate.

When deciding who sleeps on the floor, make sure your traveling companions are on the up and up. One band's drummer and guitarist conspired against the bass player, so that he always lost in the game of Rock Paper Scissors. And he never even suspected a thing.

HOTEL PSYCHOSIS

Sometimes checking out the room beforehand won't be enough to save you. Don't forget, these are rented rooms; if those walls could talk, what stories would they tell? Murder? Mayhem? These places tend to attract some really strange energy.

Once, while staying in a motel off Venice Beach, I had visions of gore and blood. I got so thoroughly spooked, I kept all the lights and television on while I paced the night away, keeping my distance from the bed where I had discovered an ominous stain beneath the sheet. Maybe someone had just gotten her period in the middle of the night. Then again, maybe not.

"What do you expect?" said the clerk, when I asked him about the room's history. "This place has been here since 1910, I'm sure that a lot of things have happened here."

CHOOSING YOUR COMPANIONS

Sometimes there is no choice, but when possible,

try to select traveling companions who are well traveled or at least laid-back. The last thing you want is a trauma child going nuts in the back seat because plans have gone askew. That's the thing: plans will always go askew, it's how you deal with the situation that's important.

It also helps if your companions are street smart. Many a roadtrip has been in danger because of city hick naiveté. Unless you absolutely trust their judgment, don't let these people party with strangers in the wilderness, ask pimps for street directions, provoke fights with the regulars, or shoot up in gas station bathrooms.

CROSSING BORDERS

This is serious business. It can either be a breeze or a long expensive hassle. When driving into Canada, we rearranged the pals in the car so the people with the most visible tattoos and piercings were in the back seat. The driver and front seat passenger brushed their hair and put on their cleanest, least scraggly sweaters. Everyone should have their I.D.s (passports or driver's licenses) out and ready to show if asked. Take off your sunglasses.

Be prepared, the least amount of time spent dealing with border guards the better. The driver should be coherent and do all of the talking. Be ready to answer questions like "Where are you going?", "How long are you staying?", "Where will you be staying?", and "Where are you from?" If you are traveling with a rock band and they ask if you have any CDs or t-shirts that you're planning to sell, tell them that they will be given away for promotional use only. Otherwise you'll wind up paying a mighty tax. Think about crossing at an alternative border entrance (e.g., the one that trucks, not tourists, use). Often the guards will be so busy with the trucks' paperwork that they'll ask a few questions and wave you on through.

The same goes for coming back into the country. Don't carry any pot. I've encountered police dogs sniffing luggage at the Minneapolis airport at 3 a.m., and everywhere else as well. The customs agents in every country do as much profiling, if not more, than cops everywhere, so dress in your nicest clothes, brush your hair and be polite. Do not make jokes. Answer questions with the fewest words possible. Smile politely. Be aware that crossing borders is an opportunity to really screw yourself up if you're not careful.

If you do get hassled, be sure to write down the names and/or badge numbers of everyone involved. Note the date and time of the interaction. Do not hesitate to ask to speak to someone's supervisor. When a customs agent or border guard is speaking, do not interrupt them. Listen closely, and when they are finished, ask whatever questions you have. Do not volunteer information, and do not sign anything ever without reading it carefully. Always carry the numbers of close people you can call collect in an emergency.

DON'T DO THIS!

Cops at 4 a.m.

Here's a cautionary tale told by an old roadtripster:

Once upon a time, we were driving from Berkeley up the coast to Seattle. Around 4 a.m. we stopped just south of Portland, Oregon for a shift change behind the wheel. Since it was my turn to drive, we conveniently had landed at an all-night Denny's where I tanked up on multiple cups of steamin' hot java. Properly wired, I was ready to put the pedal to the metal for the final sunrise haul up through the Pacific Northwest. Everyone in the car was ready to go back to sleep, and a joint was passed to get everyone settled down for the drive.

I'll be the first to admit that between the caffeine and pot and 4 a.m. buzz, I wasn't keeping as close an eye on the speedometer as maybe I should have. The highway was wide open, we were the only car in sight. Until the flashing red and blue lights appeared in the rearview mirror. Fuck. Okay, everyone, roll down the windows and get some fresh air in here. NOW.

I pull over. The cop walks up to the driver's side window, shines his flashlight around the car, says, "Do you have any more marijuana in here?"

"Uh, no," I reply, totally bumming out.

"Do you know how fast you were going?" the smarmy cop sneered.

"Uh, 55?" I suggested.

"Faster than that," he replied. "Okay, miss, I need to see your license and registration." He walks back to his patrol car clutching my paperwork. This cop can't be older than 18, I'm thinking. He's probably the new guy working the graveyard shift out on the quiet stretch of highway. He comes back.

"Please step out of the car."

I step out of the car. He asks if I've been smoking

marijuana. No. He smells marijuana in the car, he says. I start talking quickly and earnestly. Also very, very respectfully. "We're just going as far as Portland, officer. It's late and the other kids in the car took a few hits of pot to help them fall asleep hours ago. We only had one joint and it's gone. Really." Gulp.

This cop, who's barely old enough to shave, is giving me the hairy eyeball, trying to size up if I'm telling the truth. He decides to read me my rights. Until a cop has stood in front of you pronouncing, "You have the right to remain silent..." you probably wouldn't think twice about firing up a doobie in the car... Let me tell you, don't do it. In your car, you're a sitting duck for cops to swoop in and fuck with you for almost any reason. They're thinking about all the brownie points and promotions they'll get, and you're thinking, Boy, I just set myself up for the biggest hassle of my life, when a simple speeding ticket would have sufficed.

Yeah, well, at least this story had a happy ending. To make a long story short, the cop ordered everyone out of the car. Searched it, found one roach only (proof that there is a god), missed the doses, the rest of the pot and who knows what else, and let us off with a speeding ticket and a lecture. The whole time he was searching the car, I was telepathically signaling this guy that he didn't want to ruin the lives of four young people. Maybe being an even younger guy he lacked the self-confidence to bust us. Whatever it was, we were happy to be merrily on our way. And the moral of the story is: don't smoke pot in a car, because driving is one of the only times cops can hassle you without any reason at all

ROAD TRIP LITMUS TEST

You're sitting in the living room with pals when the idea of a roadtrip suddenly comes up. Ask yourself a few questions:

• Can I afford this?
• Are these people talking bullshit?
• Can they handle being in the car with me for a few days?
• Can I handle being in the car with them for a few days?
• Where are we going?
• How well does the car run?
• Is there a modicum of responsibility in any of these people?
• Do I care?

WHEN DISASTER STRIKES

Traveling with someone can be a bonding experience or an exercise in hatred and futility. Survival instincts are needed to rise above petty differences; otherwise, guaranteed, someone will be shedding tears before the end of the journey and you better hope it isn't you.

If your constant need to control and dominate people is a personal problem for you, you may wonder before you get into the car whether this trip is going to work out. Maybe your companions enjoy personal psychodrama. In that case, you're just the person to give it to them. At least you'd be entertaining, and that counts for a lot on the road.

There are people out there whose main purpose in life seems to be annoying the hell out of those around them. They are ignorant of what they do, and if they do know, they don't care. This type of person is called a sociopath. They'll go on and on, prattling in some authoritative manner about the merits of Motorhead versus Queensryche, or the stock market, or public radio, or how sick they still are from the evening before. Unless, of course, the others in the car share these interests. Then it's perfectly acceptable, as Miss Manners might say.

DON'T DO THIS!

Taking the Boyfriend

One of the worst companions I ever had on a road trip also happened to be my boyfriend at the time. By the end of that trip, I was clawing at the passenger side window, praying for a way out and a way home.

There were five of us in a Nissan truck and campershell going on a cross-country trek to, of all things, a poetry competition. It was the middle of August, so we ran into a lot of heat and wet weather before we got there. The back got musty quickly and opening the back window offered little relief.

We got to Michigan, our destination, when the boyfriend became mouthy and insulting. He took over my room, got drunk, spent all his money, and was mostly a jerk. I knew then the relationship was over and I was regretting that he had even come with us.

On the way home, he was picking his nose and scratching his balls, when he reached over to me, saying, "C'mere, baby." I was repulsed, leaned all the way over to the door and avoided looking at him again after that. A few months later, when we were still working together, I would look at him and wonder if things before the road trip would ever be the same. They weren't.

Some wonderful people I know travel well together as couples. I am not one of those people. I work well alone or in packs, but I've never mastered the couples thing. The clinginess ties me up and slows me down while I like to remain cling-free.

I think couples are the most difficult combination of people to sofasurf. Don't think because you're sharing a bed that it's easy for your hosts. If anything, you are now double the pain in the ass. Lovers: if you have the budget, invest in a cheap hotel room. That way you get the bath, the bed and personal time together. If you're staying with pals, don't forget to wash the linens and discreetly throw away the used condoms. And remember to be quiet! Nobody wants to listen to the soundtrack of *New Wave Hookers III*, unless of course, they're in it.

THE FATAL FLAW

Money is one of the most evil things to fight about. People remember every financial slight or debt. Try to keep in mind that money isn't that important, certainly not worth losing pals over unless they are taking full-on advantage of you. Pool your resources.

Everyone on the road trip should make contributions to the gas tank, food and lodging. The gesture is as important as the kick. And if one of your companions is broke, lend him or her $20 if you can, buy them breakfast or a beer. Show some class.

One fair and easy way to make sure the cost of the trip is spread evenly, have every person take turns filling the gas tanks. The car's owner should not have to foot the bill, as they are already providing the means of travel.

DON'T DO THIS!

Lugging Dead Weight

Actually, the whole recipe for disaster went something like this:

Five of us went to Austin. Ellen decided to join us at the last minute, after Alice had extended an invitation. Alice and her boyfriend Bob decided then that they wanted to take another vehicle, that the Nissan truck trick was too cramped. So they rented a late-model Bronco. Did they offer to drive all five of us? No, we took two vehicles. That should have sent up a serious flare right there.

Cheater got bummed because, now, instead of splitting the cost of gas five ways, it was split between me and him. Ellen alternative rode in either vehicle and didn't offer gas money to anyone. This was another flare on the trip.

We invaded the tiny one bedroom apartment of a friend. I slept under the dining table. There were way too many people. This was another flare on the trip.

Frances, our host, was really gracious about everything, even though Ellen stayed for two extra days. Frances wouldn't have minded so much if Ellen had cleaned the kitchen or taken out the garbage or something. But she didn't. Alice was a primadonna and threw a bunch of tantrums that I posted online. Bob and Chester, they were smart and stayed the hell out of the estrogen storm. Are any of the girls in this story still friends? No.

FORMULA FOR HAPPINESS

Remember that nothing on this earth is truly yours, money comes and money goes, everything you send out into the universe will come back to you. Believe in the Cosmic Santa: We all get what we deserve.

ROAD TIP

Used Tire Shops

When you're on the road it's easy to be ripped off by those roadside garage stations. Their mechanics charge more by the hour and their products have a high markup because they figure you' re traveling and don't have a lot of options. They're right to an extent, but you can avoid getting ripped off on basic services like fixing flat tires. Roadside garages will try to sell you a brand new tire, then scare you by saying the other tires are in disrepair. This is where I think these garages try to take advantage of solo women travelers and play on their fears.

With a little help from the local yellow page directory, you can find a tire shop in the vicinity that will sell you a used tire for $20 or less. It'll save you about $50 and the tire will get you home until you can take care of it.

FAMILY ROAD TRIPS

Why do people continue to make their lives miserable with family pilgrimages? It's tolerable as a young child, but the ritual sometimes carries into adulthood. People have a short memory, it's true, because before we know it, there we go again getting into the car with the people we call family.

While riding in a Volkswagen van in the mountains outside of Oaxaca, my brother and sister were retching in the back, my grandparents were stoically bearing up under it all while my mother cursed a blue streak. Later that night, in Oaxaca, it was New Year's Eve but it didn't even matter because no one was speaking to each other. Yow! What a terrible dinner that was.

Another time there I was with the family (no one learned the lessons before, short memory strikes again) in New York City. The hostility got so intense, with no one speaking to each other or even having a good time, that we cut the vacation short two weeks so everyone could return to their respective homes. We never did make it to Florida. My mother and I went to Puerto Rico a couple of years later. I got sick with the flu the first day and I remember very vividly saying, "Send me home, I made a mistake!"

My grandparents had already traveled the world, but it was always done in tour groups so they were conditioned to be dependent on other people to take them places and make decisions. Don't do that to your traveling companions or tolerate that from them. No one wants to be wearing the tour guide hat during a road trip, everyone should be contributing to the success of the trip.

HITCHHIKING

Normally, don't do it. Women should NEVER hitch alone. Ever. If you feel safe, you aren't carrying much stuff, then go ahead and stick your thumb out. If you're broken down, it may be a necessity. It's safer for men than for women, but women have an easier time of getting rides. My experience in hitchhiking is, these people have an ulterior motive in picking you up, even if it is masked in euphemisms like "lunch" and "date." Women seldom pick up hitchhikers. Black and Latino men are usually the most courteous, white guys usually pitch the proposition. Don't get into a car with two or more men. Use common sense.

It's generally safer hitchhiking in the morning (most people don't start drinking hard before noon). If you're hitching with a buddy, it's a lot easier to get out of potentially awkward or dangerous situations.

In some parts of the country, like Taos or the Alaskan-Canada Highway, hitchhiking is a part of the local custom. This isn't necessarily the case outside of rural areas. Observe the local customs. Make sure you know where the inside door handle and lock are before you get in the car. (Check it out when the door is open. If the door handle or lock is missing or broken, pass on the ride.) At any time, if the vibe is weird, get out of the car. Trust your intuition. Refuse any ride that gives you the creeps. No matter what.

Don't ever, ever let a ride know your real destination - get dropped a block or two off center if you can.

TALKING TO STRANGERS

Don't tell strangers more than they need to know. They don't need to know your destination, the number of people in your car, or even your real name. I know it sounds rude, but predators prey off polite people. Be aware of your surroundings, use your instincts. Nosy people are to be regarded with some suspicion, you might be getting played.

DON'T DO THIS!

Tony the Rapist

It's funny how easy it is to forget your own advice sometimes. Once, in Portland, I was walking home from a club downtown, coming back across the river. This stranger I had met earlier on the street bumming a cigarette decided that he would walk with me. ("We're going in the same direction, aren't we?" he said.) We walked across the bridge, and he was creeping me out, so I decided to play it cool because it was late, the streets were bereft of cops or cabs, so I had no real choice in the matter but to go through this walk and try to appeal to this person's higher power.

Higher power? What I was thinking, I'll never know. Maybe I was still carrying the last smoldering coals of hope for humanity. I know better now.

This creep, he starts talking about how he had been raped by a woman at gunpoint. ("What would you do? If you were raped, I mean?" he asked.) He talked about his kids, he talked about a lot of things which to this day I'm still trying to recollect. I kept asking him about his children, hoping they would provide a buffer for this conversation. I asked him about his relationship with his mother, his obligations as a father, his favorite baseball team. In short, I brought up God, Mom and baseball. I tried to be that compassionate ear that so many people need once in a while. Boy, was I a sucker.

The funny thing is, I saw it coming, only at a weird angle. I just had to figure a way out of the situation without sounding off the klaxon alarm; after all, there was no one to hear it in the deserted Portland night. The worst thing, I figured, was to run. I'm just not that fast.

When he actually did make his move by putting me in a headlock, I tried to be calm and wondered if he intended to kill me too. At that very moment I was envisioning my death, a homeless person came out the shadows, oblivious to what's was going on. But he provided enough of a distraction for the creep to release me. ("Just playin'," he said.) I broke away fast, walking not running, to the place where I was staying while constantly checking over my shoulder to see if this guy was going to follow me.

If I had a gun at the time, I probably would have shot him and not felt too sorry for it, either.

I didn't know the nature of the neighborhood I was walking in, I should have stayed on streets that had people, I should have gone the opposite direction when I saw this person coming, but most of all, I should have called a taxi.

Don't go wandering around unfamiliar city neighborhoods, especially after dark, unless a local pal gives you the okay. One of my buddies mentioned that when she was growing up in New York, all of the gals carried a $20 bill folded small, tucked away in their wallets for emergency "Get-me-the-fuck-out-of-here-now" cab rides. That money was never spent ever, because it had to be there in an emergency. Not a bad idea when hanging out in a big (or small) city, no matter how familiar it may be.

GOOD GRIEF!
NOW WHAT THE FUCK WAS THAT SCENE ALL ABOUT?!
THOSE PEOPLE ARE NUTS!

TOENAILS AND COCKROACHES

JON LONGHI

If you have weird habits, do your best to keep them hidden. Your hosts may not understand. I remember a conversation I once had with my friend Miles. He was telling me about how he collects his toenails. Whenever he clips his nails he saves them in a little metal box. He's been doing this for a couple of years and has amassed quite a pile of them. (I've seen it.) When he has enough clippings he plans to do a self-portrait of himself in toenails by gluing them to a piece of paper. Miles knows someone who does exquisite illustrations in dried noodles and has talked to him about commissioning a portrait.

"It gets kind of weird and difficult when I travel," Miles told me. "Like recently I went to this family reunion in Texas. The whole time I was there I saved my toenail clippings in a little vial and then brought them back to California with me. But it would have been really hard to explain if one of my family members caught me doing that."

"What if they stopped you at the border and thought the vial was filled with some kind of drug?" I postulated. "It would have been a bummer to get thrown into jail for suspicion of smoking toenail clippings."

"Yeah, it would have been hard to convince the cops that I needed them for my art," Miles replied.

One of the most common things one has to deal with when traveling is the presence of unexpected bugs in the places they stay. The only time in my life I got crabs, they came from a couch, not a lover. On the road, one often finds themselves spending the night in a place they would never choose to live in. But it is important to not let your host know how you actually feel about their place. Be polite on all occasions. Even if it's little more than a one bedroom toilet bowl, you should let your host know that to you, it's the Ritz Carlton.

Once I was with a crowd of musicians sitting in this seedy living room drinking beer and smoking until four a.m. Despite the animation of the conversation, I noticed the house had critters. Roaches crawled up the walls and moved in the shadows. As everyone drifted home or off to bed, I was assigned the least saggy of the couches.

I asked our host, Billy, if I could have a glass of water. I wanted to drink something before I went to sleep. We got up and headed toward the kitchen. All night long I had noticed that the door to the kitchen was padded around the edges with taped on cardboard so that it closed in an almost airtight manner. I had idly wondered what this modification was for. Billy switched on the lights in the pitch black room. We walked over to the sink. And I understood what the padding on the door was for. It acted like a kind of dam.

Every inch of the sink and counter was covered with the crawling bodies of roaches. They were everywhere, covering every surface. So many of them were crawling about simultaneously that the whole room seemed to shimmer and shiver and I felt like I was having an LSD flashback. Every step I took mashed five or six of them. As I stared at the seething movement on the counter, I noticed that the roaches had different sizes, colors, and shapes to their bodies, like there were dozens of different species represented in this kitchen. I've seen bad infestations before, but this one took the cake.

Billy walked up to the cabinet and opened it. Inside, roaches crawled all over the lined up glasses. He pulled out a glass that only had about three or four roaches on it and began to wash it out in the sink. I half expected to see bugs spray from the faucet. This simple act of water use on Billy's part had washed the poor souls of seven roaches down the drain to their deaths. He filled the glass from the tap and handed it to me. I gratefully accepted the glass, but didn't take a sip from it.

Instead, I said goodnight and walked into the bathroom to get ready for bed. Once I got the door closed, I poured the water down the toilet. I washed out the last beer bottle I had drunk from and used it as a water glass. After swallowing three aspirin with sixteen ounces of H_2O, I filled the beer bottle up with water and set it next to my sleeping bag. I like to keep a glass of water next to my bed at night and drink from it when I wake up from bad dreams. I reasoned that the design of the bottle and its smooth glass edges would keep roaches from crawling up the side of it. That night I had nightmares about thousands of tiny legs tickling me.

Shortly after dawn, I got up to take a piss. I carried my beer bottle full of water into the bathroom to down a couple more aspirin to fight off what was already a throbbing hangover. As I swigged the bitter white pills down, I noticed a couple dark bodies floating in the water. I jerked the beer bottle away from my mouth and held it up to my eyes. Two roaches floated in the water, a little black one and a big brown one. The little one was dead, but the big brown one was still alive. Not only was he alive, but he was doing the backstroke. Funny thing was, something about the bug's expression made him look like he was smiling. Grinning. Like his grossing me out was just him pulling a gag or something. A practical joke. He didn't think it was so funny when I flushed him down the toilet.

HOME

BRUCE JACKSON

I was living in my car again, sleeping out by the ocean on a street with no houses. I had about fifty tapes, a walkman, an old manual typewriter, and enough excess bullshit to keep me occupied for the half an hour or so it took to fall asleep every night in a car about half the size of a Greyhound shit stall. 'Bug' was definitely the appropriate name for my four wheels. 'Rat' would have implied a size much larger than the four feet of back seat I was squeezing into each night and adjusting to livable by folding down seats and opening windows. I was just barely comfortable, and when people would walk by giving me a look to shrink me a little more, I would smile at first, but as time passed and I realized I was home and vanishing in my rearview mirror, the only way I knew of to keep from disappearing altogether was to move, so I moved.

CAR CAMPING

This is what you do if you can't sofasurf but you have wheels. It's also what you do when you are traveling without a hotel room budget.

There are places in every city where car campers converge. Avoid metered parking. Don't make your nest too obvious to passersby. Don't live too long like this, it isn't very healthy.

PARKING YOUR HOUSE

When traveling, you can have an easy night at a rest stop. The thing I notice is that mostly men stay at rest stops for the night, so I can only recommend rest stops if you're traveling with someone.

Sometimes it can get spooky when traveling alone, and I'll park for the night in a church parking lot. People seldom go looking for trouble there. If I'm on a deserted stretch of road, I'll often go down a side road and park out of view of the main highway.

SHOWERS

Fresh showers are available for about $3 at any truck stop. If you're in a city where you know a few people, you can use the shower as the perfect excuse for visiting your pals on a regular basis. Cities usually have public swimming pools which charge cheap fees (the locker rooms have showers). YMCAs also have semi-reasonable day-use fees which include showers.

AT NIGHT

Make sure you have a good sleeping bag or blanket. Blankets are better for car camping because sleeping bags tended to sleep funky after a while. Blankets are easier to air out and care for. Make sure that you're warm enough at night, because you won't be able to run your heater all night. Running the engine makes you susceptible to carbon monoxide poisoning. Also, don't sleep in the same clothes you've been wearing all day. It's an easy way to get an infection. Skin needs to breathe.

AMENITIES OF CAR CAMPING

Keep a thermos handy. Coffee can cost, but you can use a thermos to keep hot water for tea, ramen noodles, and instant oatmeal. Your diet is in danger as a car camper. You'll fight the urge on a daily basis to drive through for a Whopper instead of whipping up some hummus. Try to eat at least one decent meal a day. Fruits (apples, oranges, berries, bananas), veggies that don't have to be cooked (tomatoes, carrots, cucumbers, etc.), and a loaf of bread are cheaper than a meal at McDonald's. Find the grocery store and deal with it.

CAR CAMPING GROCERY LIST

Forget stuff that needs to be refrigerated like cheese and other dairy products. This is what I usually take for extended road trips on a tight budget:

Bread/bagels
Jelly
Water
Crackers/rice cakes
Peanut Butter
Raisins
Nuts
Apples/oranges

COMMUNICATING FROM THE ROAD

If you have the luxury of a laptop computer, cyberspace is the answer. There are several national and regional companies that offer flat rate Internet service. Sometimes a generous friend may let you use their account, so you can send e-mail while jumping from city to city but it makes retrieving e-mail nearly impossible.

If you are highly mobile, you aren't going to have any time to set up cybershop. Call your pals collect, invest in a prepaid phone card (19 cents a minute is reasonable), invest in postcards. People still have sentimental feelings for snail mail, there's a lot of charm and romance and something tangible about it.

Keep an active mailbox somewhere. Have a reliable friend pick up your mail and pay your bill. An official United States Postal Service P.O. Box costs $40/year, a lot less than a mailbox service place (approximately $6/month). In some cities, more stable friends let me use their home addresses. The only problem is keeping in contact. There is some mail you will never see using this method.

CAMPER'S READING LIST

Road Tested Books

The characteristics of a good road book include a spellbinding story that will keep a reader glued for many, many hours on a Greyhound bus, yet can be shut and re-opened on a dime ("Yikes! That's my stop!!!" or my flight, or my ride, or...). It should give your mind something substantial to chew on while taking a shift behind the wheel at 4 a.m. It should keep you company when things get a little lonely, like when you find yourself in a coffeeshop with a couple of hours to kill in a strange town, or maybe your hosts need to reclaim their space for the afternoon. A good road book gives you a sense of being someplace, even when you're nowhere at all.

On The Road by Jack Kerouac
Fear and Loathing In Las Vegas by Hunter S. Thompson
Electric Kool Aid Acid Test by Tom Wolfe
Confederacy of Dunces by John Kennedy Toole
100 Years of Solitude by Gabriel Garcia Marquez
Geek Love by Katherine Dunn
Moon is a Harsh Mistress by Robert Heinlein
Childhood's End by Arthur C. Clarke
Motorcycle Diaries by Che Guevara
Atlas Shrugged by Ayn Rand
Magic Journey by John Nichols

As much as I love horror and the occult, I don't recommend reading H.P. Lovecraft while you are sleeping in your car in the middle of nowhere.

DON'T DO THIS!

Mardi Gras Grand Theft Auto

Every con man and thief from the South converges on New Orleans during Mardi Gras. And why not? The pickings are easy. I knew this going in, so I don't have anyone to blame for what happened:

I got great parking in the French Quarter. I slept in the Jeep since I didn't have hotel reservations anywhere, and the nearest available room was 60 miles north in Baton Rouge. A great time was had with a bunch of new pals, all of whom where too drunk to trust. But the Jeep, it's really easy to break into, and sometime during the festivities someone stole all my stuff, leaving behind only the rock that they used to break in with.

I went to the police station to report it. I knew the stuff was long gone, but I figured that the city could use the statistic. There was a girl inside, talking to the clerk.

"What are you here for?" she asked me.

"All my stuff got ripped off out of my car," I told her. "What about you?"

"My car got ripped off, with all my stuff inside!"

Turned out that she was car camping, and someone came along while she was partying and stole the car. She was totally stranded, her hometown was Cincinnati. If I had the money I would have bought her a beer and a bus ticket home.

PARKING TICKETS

It was easier to be a parking criminal five years ago. Now that most major cities have installed major computer systems to chart the flow of parking tickets, you can rest assured that they will track down your illegally-parked sorry ass across the country. Then the fines won't double either. They triple, and sometimes, quadruple.

Best thing is to watch the signs and obey obey obey. Los Angeles charges $60 for some parking violations, San Francisco will tow your car, and Seattle will send nasty letters to your house.

Eventually all the unpaid fines get turned over to a collection agency that has all the time in the world to stuff your mailbox with demands for retribution. It's been a big ugly mess since major cities have come to depend on parking fines as a means of revenue.

Some cities have alternative means for dealing with parking tickets. San Francisco has 'Project 20', where a person can sign up for community service instead of forking over a heap of cash. Find the right non-profit and those parking ticket problems are resolved in a jiffy.

TRAFFIC CITATIONS

Contest these if you are planning on staying in town. Sometimes you can get them dismissed if the officer fails to show up (a more common occurrence than the judicial system cares to admit). That way, it never gets on your record and you don't have to pay the increased insurance. Sometimes you can exchange the fines for community service. Sometimes you can spend the day in 'traffic school'. Otherwise you will have to pay, and if you don't, the judge issues a bench warrant for your arrest and you'll have to pay a beefy fine anyway.

NO, I'LL JUST LIE HERE FOR AWHILE
AND COUNT THE MINUTES... WAIT TILL
MORNING..... THEN I'LL ..... I'LL ....

OUTRAGEOUS FORTUNE

BRUCE JACKSON

I lived in my car for three months. I kept a ten-dollar bill in my pocket at all times to keep from feeling like a bum. I listened to the radio a lot (only talk). I listened to music only on tapes. I bought a bus pass to get around town. I parked a block from a layover zone. I only moved my car on street cleaning days.

I found a job that had a shower. I shit before I left work. I parked beside a public toilet just in case. (It closed at ten.) I showered in the morning before work. I brought a change of clothes with me. I changed clothes before work.

I typed stories on the park bench near my car. Police always fuck with you when you're in the middle of writing something good in public.

I signed up for Roommate Referral. Nobody wanted me. I kept looking. I liked living in my car, but it wasn't very comfortable. The cops didn't like me.

They gave me tickets for living in my car. I gave them fake names.

I showered at the beach on weekends. The water was very cold. I showered at the university when I could. I shit wherever I could on weekends. Mostly I shit at the mall. I used the telephone at the bus depot. I almost never shit there.

I hung out at coffeeshops. I smoked, and made wire sculptures. I beat off at Don's 99-channel Video Arcade on Sixth Street. I didn't buy any drugs. I saved a lot of money.

I grew comfortable with myself. I stayed signed up with Roommate Referral. I found a place to live. I took a nice long bath the day I moved in. I still take baths. I took a nice long shit the day I moved in. I still shit. I still had my ten-dollar bill when I moved into my new place. I gave my car away a month later.

I would have written this on that park bench, but it's gone.

MODERN NOMADICS

Certain destinations have distinguished themselves among sofa-surfing aficionados. Whether it's a sight of tremendous beauty, a wild party, or a singular not-to-be-missed experience, a few are included here to whet that travelin' appetite, and inspire forays into exploring the truth that is out there.

There's a ton of stuff to check out, actually. The roses in Portland, Oregon (which also has a cool hip-hop festival in June). The Tibetan Freedom Concert, wherever it is (all-star lineup, watch out for lightning). The Oregon Shakespeare Festival in Ashland. The Gay, Lesbian Bi-Sexual & Transgender Parade in San Francisco in late June. Halloween on Hollywood Boulevard in Los Angeles. The tourist kitsch of Venice Beach. Yosemite National Park. Free wine-tasting at the vineyards of Napa Valley. Garage Shock in Bellingham, Washington. Carlsbad Caverns in New

Mexico. Shiprock and the Four Corners area. The Rainbow Gathering (every summer in a national park, visit www.welcomehome.org for info).

Remember, every city and many small towns offer free concerts and performances in their parks during the summer, as well as free days at the museums and zoos. Look in the local paper, or call the museum directly for time of free or reduced admissions. Just because you're living cheap doesn't mean you can't live well... Volunteer to usher at a local theater and enjoy free performances of opera, ballet, music, and theater. Enjoy, enjoy!

HOW TO GET IN FREE

Two ways: either sneak in underneath the fence or volunteer to work the show. If it's a benefit for a non-profit, the organizers are almost always looking for volunteers. Plus it's way more fun to work a show than to pay full price or get your knees all dirty and risk getting busted. At big festivals, the key to getting in early is showing up before the gates open and seeing if any of the food vendors need extra hands to carry stuff and set up. The production crew is so busy running around, they don't have time to pay attention, and most will think that you're with one of the vendors. Stay out of the way. If you're walking around without a purpose, the security guys running the perimeters will be sure to stop and say good morning to gauge what your business is.

NEW ORLEANS

Mardi Gras and Jazz Fest

Mardi Gras is also known as Fat Tuesday, and it always occurs the day before Lent begins. But the partying starts way in advance in New Orleans, as mighty throngs descend into town for revelry and hijinx. Parades, bawdiness, and fun are in order. Be careful (see page 88) but at least once in your life, try and check it out. The citywide New Orleans Jazz Festival is a city that never sleeps but keeps things shaking all night and way past the dawn. Nonstop music and partying - some of the best this country has to offer.

HAPPY CAMPER TIPS

New Orleans

- Don't go into graveyards alone, especially at night.
- Don't go down deserted streets in the French Quarter, they are usually deserted for a reason.
- Don't bring anything you aren't willing to lose.
- Don't leave your drink unattended.
- Don't flash your money, especially traveler's checks. It screams tourist.
- Don't wear expensive jewelry, it's only asking for unwanted attention.

WALT'S WORLD

Disneyland

The Happiest Place on Earth continues to a magnet for funlovers. But it wears a mask, like any other place.

Go early, stay late, get your money's worth. Go on a weekday when kids are in school. Lots of cheap motels surround the place. For tawdry details about the dark side of Mousetown, please refer to John Marr's excellent zine *Murder Can be Fun*. In the meantime, a former roommate offered her own personal experience:

She went to Disneyland a few years back with some coworkers. They were in the park already and returned to their car to spark up a joint. Well, let me tell you now that Disneyland and its surrounding grounds are covered with state-of-the-art surveillance that is comparable to the Pentagon. Well, anyway, to make a long story short, all of a sudden this guy appears dressed in faux military apparel, banging on her window and yelling for them to get out of the car. There were three other guys with him, all in radio contact with homebase ("Check the floor of the car, it looks like they dropped something.") While one of the Disneypolice was playing bad cop with my roommate, the other cop is having a lively discussion with my roomie's friend. The nice guy cop is filling out a standard formatted Disney crime checklist that includes murder, rape, and incest. ("Oh, yeah," says the Good Cop, "You wouldn't believe some of the things we see here. It's a whole other world.")

ELVIS LIVES!

Graceland

When anywhere near Memphis... Graceland is great. Skip the aeroplane tour and just do the house.

They don't let you upstairs, so no bedrooms and toilets but the most of it is pretty campy fun, but be careful, cos if you happen to utter anything disrespectful, old white trash tourist women with flabby arms will pummel you. Go on weekdays, less people to irritate. Buy your postcards (use the machine where they'll superimpose you and your loved one's mug onto the postcard, why not!) and send it there cos they'll use their special Graceland stamp chop to postmark all your mail! Wow!

SCENIC SERENITY

Alaska-Canada Highway

This road is the stunning connector to the 49th state. It's paved nearly all the way, though I hear it closes in the middle of winter. That makes sense, actually, it would be terrible to have car trouble in such a desolate place.

First thing you do, before you've left the States, is get your car checked over by a trusted mechanic. Next, buy a Milepost, which is the mile-by-mile map of the highway. It's very explicit, it runs about $15, but you'll be happy about that later when you're on the road wondering just how far it is to the next gas station.

I went in the summer. My Jeep had suffered a major car breakdown in Spokane, so I was already apprehensive. But the nice thing about summer is all the daylight hours you get, particularly in that part of the world. Summer daylight can last as long as 20 hours. So it makes driving a lot easier. I was able to knock off 600, 700 miles in a day. Ooooo-weeee!!!

There are some places to stay along the way, but

the weather is so nice that it's easy to just pull out the sleeping bag and sleep in the back seat. I just got on a side road, not too far from the beaten path in case I broke down again, but far enough so I wasn't visible from the road.

Make time to stop and enjoy some of the sights along the Al-Can Highway, especially Laird Hot Springs, that place alone is practically worth the drive.

Chaco Canyon

Chaco Canyon is the kind of place where all the mysteries of the universe seem to be lurking in the valley's crumbled ruins and red stone cliffs. The place is so quiet and serene that you can hear your soul breathing. It's remote. A slow, nerve-wracking drive of 30 to 50 miles through a rugged desert on a line of pot holes, washouts, and bowling-ball-sized rocks weeds out all the idiots. There's no excess of loud gaudy tourists to mar the exquisite views. Centuries ago, an advanced Native American civilization lived in the canyon. They built intricate stone buildings around the valley, the ruins of which remain. Chaco Canyon is the ultimate place for transcendental epiphanies and camping out beneath the endless stars.

Joshua Tree in April

In the desert between L.A. and Las Vegas is Joshua Tree National Monument. In April, the cacti bloom in surreal formations and the desert floor, usually a barren monochromatic scene, explodes into a psychedelic carpet of wildflowers. Truly an amazing sight to behold - nature at its finest - the desert in bloom!

On the way to Joshua Tree from L.A., there's the little town of Cabazon, where they have these humongous dinosaurs as seen in the Pee Wee Herman movie. The store is in the T-Rex and you climb up his butt to get to it. Yay!!!!

Hot Springs

When you're driving around America, there must be a better excuse to get out of the car to stretch your legs than just another cup of coffee at the next truckstop. One of the greatest excuses for getting sidetracked is hot springs, which pop up all over the darn place once you start paying attention. Some are highly developed with paved parking lot, admission fees, and swimming pool type arrangements, but plenty are just a follow-the-dirt-path to natural pools of hot water, usually next to a river or stream. Having a relaxing soak in a hot spring renews one's spirit, and can restore even the most burnt-out roadtrippers.

START YOUR ENGINES

The Indy 500

It's one of the biggest tailgate parties in the nation. A week before, the campers and RVs are arriving to find a decent parking space. The night before the Big Race, there's a promenade on the strip outside the raceway where drunk revelers are hollering at women to "Show us yer tits!" Sigh. Hey, what did you expect?

Like Mardi Gras, you're going to need to make hotel reservations early. The best way to experience this American tradition is through the eyes of a local pal, who can explain the history and traditions. Plus they know where the best parties are.

It's all a big party, full of gearheads and bikers, racers and groupies. If you go a few days early you can catch qualifying races, which is a much cheaper ticket than the Big Race.

BEST OUTDOOR CONCERT VENUES

Redrocks Amphitheater Boulder. Colorado

The Gorge at George. Washington

The world is full of places like the Nassau Coliseum or the Philly Spectrum or (fill in the name of the big concert stadium in your hometown). Big deal. You're there to see the band, not the scenery. Unless, of course, you're at Redrocks, an outdoor amphitheater located in the mountain desert near Boulder. The sandstone formations are spectacular and provide amazing enhancement to any musical experience. Same goes for the Gorge, an outdoor amphitheater located on the rim of the Columbia River Gorge in eastern Washington. Few places combine the brilliance of enormous human talent - the music - with nature's absolute majesty. If you're anywhere near one of these places, catch a show if there are still tickets available. Even if it's Yanni opening for Barney the purple dinosaur.

FESTIVAL FUN

Int'l Albuquerque Balloon Festival

The beautiful International Albuquerque Balloon

Festival happens in October. Six hundred hot-air balloons go up every morning over the fields and mesas for about two weeks. There are evening exhibitions, and daily lift-off races and you could even participate by being on a chase crew that follows the balloon's progress. It's absolutely gorgeous. Santa Fe Fiestas happens right around Labor Day weekend. It's a twisted celebration of the war between people in Northern New Mexico, but the pyrotechnic display is awesome.

South By Southwest

The biggest music festival in the United States happens at South By Southwest in Austin every March. Fifty venues, eight bands each, lasts a week if you go early for the indie film festival. Austin is the coolest city in Texas, and a bit of an art and music Southern mecca for its cheap rents, UT-Austin and laid back nature. Richard Linklater's *Slacker* didn't deviate too much from the reality, though corporate money is creeping into the scene, the newest Silicon Valley is just over the hill, and change is on the horizon. (Kind of like what happened to Seattle, though I still love that town.) SXSW has since extended the tentacles of their influence to Portland and St. Louis, sponsoring music festivals in those cities as well. The *College Music Journal* has been sponsoring their own music festival in NYC for quite a number of years. On the web, find out more at www.cmjmusic.com.

Bumbershoot

In Seattle, the big festival is Bumbershoot, which happens Labor Day weekend. It features more than twenty stages showcasing traditional and avant-garde performance art, literary readings and music music music late into the evening. Where else can you see Sonic Youth and Ted Joans, Eileen Myles and Mudhoney, Dorothy Allison and L7, Eric Bogosian and Gas Huffer? Not all on the same stage, of course, but you get the idea. It tends to be extremely crowded, but you get a lot for a $10 all-day admission.

ComiCon

The grandma of all the comix conventions, the ComiCon, happens every August in San Diego. Not only is it a mega trade show with all your fave superheroes and underground characters, but it's also open to the public for buying and selling antiquated comics and original art by notorious lowbrow artists. Similar regional conventions are held through out the country. Keep your eyes out and get that outfit of *Too Much Coffee Man* ready. Dressing up always adds to the party, even if it is in some hangar-style building. There are even some jobs available at these affairs that will pay you to wear some costume, ranging from Spiderman to the Rugrats. Call your favorite comix label. They're always up for a good laugh, you'd be surprised.

BURNING MAN'S COUCH
by Stephen Spyrit

So you want to crash on Burning Man's couch... You've heard some whispers about it or maybe saw coverage on a major network. Ten thousand strangers: just add water and stir, garnish with a 60-foot flaming exploding effigy! It's a true global collection of people and all forms of art. Participation is the only method - this is not a spectator sport but there is plenty to watch.

Well, first you'll have to bring your own couch. On your back, in an RV, strapped on your car or go totally metaphor and crash on the ground. Be realistic when figuring where you fall on the feral curve: RV being up around ten, and sleeping with dust for a blanket in the zero range. The site of Burning Man, Black Rock City, is on a lake that couldn't take the neighborhood and died.

Living on I-5, I had heard of the Man for years, driving though at the end of '93, and the pre-Man of '96. '97 was my first start-to-finish Burning Man. Every year is different. If you don't have it at home, go to the library for internet access - it's free and easy. On the www.burningman.com page, click on must read survivals. What you MUST bring on any trip to the desert (Burning Man or otherwise):

- 2 gallons of water per person per day. Keep a bottle of water with you at all times.
- enough food/beverages and ice for your entire party.
- first aid kit.
- bedding and shelter of some type; the winds can reach 50 mph (a good camp tent is recommended along with warm sleeping bags.)
- each vehicle should bring a shovel.
- garbage bags.
- any required prescriptions, contact lens supplies (disposables work great), or whatever else you need to maintain your health and comfort in a remote area with no services.

Also recommended:

- sunscreen/sunblock lotion and sunglasses. Shade structures, umbrellas, parasols, hats, sheets; the sun wants you!
- a cooking stove if you expect to heat food or liquid.
- flashlights and spare batteries.
- bicycles (mountain bikes or cruisers; with balloon tires are best).
- ear plugs! (not everyone is going to want to sleep when you do).
- warm clothes for cold desert nights.
- heavy ziploc bags for cameras or electronic gear you may bring.
- lotion, lip balm, insect repellent.

Costumes, musical instruments, props, banners, signs, and anything else you can think of that might make the experience more fun for you and your Playa neighbors. Most of all, bring common sense, an open mind, and a positive attitude.

These are real must-brings, no bullshit, no one can bigmacnipulate a way out of it. Just the exercise of existing beyond the apron strings of mother culture for a few days is worth the price of admission. Bitching about the admission price ($100) requires sitting down and having a nice chat about all the stupid ways money is manipulated out of everyone and the few ways money is used to further yourself and those around you. It's not a get rich kind of event, the production costs are staggering: there's the bloodthirsty county, all the building and clean-up, you name it. If you don't have the money but still want to go, get in touch with the organizers (check the website for how to do that) and volunteer. In lieu of cash, commit some of your time and energy to make Burning Man happen.

It's about the burn but it's water, the elixir of life and the miracle of our little blue planet that dictates the pleasure index. Be an H_2O angel and bring some to share with strangers!! Many of the theme camps and small clusters of group campers have porta showers - such an opulent display can make you drool by day three. Stripping crowds follow the water trucks that drive through Black Rock City to settle the dust and sprinkle the populace. Gleefully I ran from the shade each day when lucky enough to catch the truck. Transpo to the hot springs can put you in touch with Momma Nature's first hot tubs. We left with a wait 'til next year enthusiasm, this in a car of cynical NW writers. That's always a good sign. Traveling in a pack, however small, is always preferred. Much easier to bring just one or two bikes and share, food and water is easier to care for the more people there, plus you have someone to share "Did you see..." questions with.

Try It Thoughts

nude body paint green and detailed to look like county sheriffs - solar cooker or flat bread bakery - mariachi band - packing out more trash than they made - kites, more kites! - hand fans - zip together 10 sleeping bags and invite some friends - solar radio - finding thirsty people and giving them water - glow in the dark clothes - bring your Art to trade or give away - lots of fruit

MAN, WHAT A JOKE. MY ONE SHOT AT THE "BIG TIME", AND LOOK WHERE IT GOT ME — COLD AND WET IN A SMALL TOWN BUS STATION IN THE MIDDLE OF THE NIGHT...
BOARDING NOW FOR THE 11:55 TO SEATTLE...

GETTING FROM POINT A TO POINT B

PART ONE - BUSES

WHY THE BUS?

I don't have to decide what I'm doing until the day of departure. Then all I have to do is show up an hour before the bus leaves and all is good. There's almost always a seat on a Greyhound bus. Also, it's cheap, and even cheaper if you buy the tickets three weeks in advance.

GETTING A GOOD SEAT

You'll see a wide range of humanity at the Greyhound bus station. Watch your belongings and don't get too comfortable, particularly at the Los Angeles station. Avoid getting a bus seat anywhere near children (unless you have them), because eventually, you can bet, they're gonna shriek like banshees. The further you are away from it, the better. Unless you like kids. Then, by all means, knock yourself out entertaining them so the rest of us can get some sleep.

To travel in comfort on Greyhound, take a blanket and a small travel pillow, if you have it. Also, eyeshades are useful. When the driver makes a stop in the middle of the night, the bus driver turns on all the lights. Ugh.

Always go for the window seat, that way people won't be repeatedly bumping into you. Don't sit in the back of the bus. That's where the drunks hang out so they can sneak drinks from brown paper bags out of the watchful eye of the driver who will kick them off if he catches them. Plus, let's get real, that bathroom begins to stink to high heaven after the second day on the bus. And avoid sitting too close to the front. That's where the talkers hang out, they usually have something going on with the bus driver.

GETTING LUCKY

No, not that way. Sometimes you'll get lucky and have both seats to yourself. Be happy but not an asshole about it. Don't act like one of those little old ladies who sits on the outside with an ugly look on her face like she's daring you to sit next to her. Unless, in your heart, you really are a grumpy old lady, then go right ahead and give everyone a dirty look.

GREASY SPOONS

Your food intake is going to be limited to overpriced bus station greasy spoons and fast food joints. The best thing to do is to stock up on food before you go to the station. Even convenience food will be cheaper than the prices that you'll face on the Greyhound route (as expensive as it is, it's not nearly as expensive as airport food).

Avoid the deli foods at the convenience stores along the bus route. You don't know how long that food has been there, and there will be only yourself and your busmates to deal with that dose of botulism.

If you want to treat yourself extra special, take a thermos of coffee. The driver knows where the good coffee is, and many of the pit stops the driver makes will brew a fresh pot of coffee on his arrival.

Also, if the driver makes an extended meal stop at a diner while saying, "These are the best hotcakes on the interstate," take his word for it and order a short stack. It's his route, and we're just traveling on it.

BUS BATHROOM

Use the fast food restrooms instead of the bathroom in the back of the bus. I guess, at the beginning of the trip, it's okay, but guaranteed, the fast food bathrooms are a lot cleaner. In the bag that you carry on board (the heavier luggage is stowed underneath the bus), make sure to include a hairbrush, a toothbrush, and soap. Antiseptic towelettes or baby wipes are key, especially in warm weather.

BIGBRO IS WATCHING

Once, while on a Greyhound bus on my way out of El Paso, the bus was stopped at a check point on Interstate 10 and boarded by INS agents who proceeded to ask the passengers about their citizenship. How rude! How unconstitutional! I think it smacks of racism, to boot.

I have also heard that Greyhound allows the DEA to board buses with dogs sometimes, but I have not witnessed that.

FITTING THE CRIMINAL PROFILE

The latest criminal profile making waves through the law enforcement agencies targets young women traveling alone. If you are like me, expect to be hassled at least once. I suppose looking ethnic doesn't help. The best thing to do, DON'T CARRY ANYTHING. Especially marijuana. It's the most bulky, odorous thing to carry. If you have to, be discrete. If you can't be discrete, be careful. Some bus drivers are cool and ignore that special smell you bring on the bus, others will kick you off and call the cops. If you have to carry herb because you are so chronic, then wait to smoke it until you reach your destination.

Or better, bake brownies prior to leaving. Nibbling on pot brownies can do wonders for any lengthy trip, just watch the quantity consumed. They may taste so good, you'll conk out completely and end up in a not-so-great situation.

ALTERNATIVE BUS LINES

I recommend the West Coast bus line Green Tortoise. The Green T is the only commercial bus line with sleeper bunks. The bus runs primarily from Seattle to Los Angeles, but it also has a ton of scheduled trips to Yosemite, Alaska, Mexico, and beyond. The ticket on the main line runs about $60, and the bus stops at the home camp in Oregon where everyone helps to make dinner and frolic naked in the river. It's a great ride if you're into camaraderie, and the passengers are always interesting. Their number is 1-800-TORTOIS.

On the East Coast, try Explorer Bus Lines at 1-800-210-2680.

Rapidos Turismos runs from Los Angeles to El Paso, Albuquerque and Denver. It's about $30, and the buses have movies. I got to watch Die Harder with Spanish subtitles. The clientele is mostly Spanish-speaking, so if you're a female traveling alone, be aware of the cultural bias that may be thrown your way. I chose to be quiet and covered my tattoos. My Spanish is terrible, which didn't help matters much.

If you are trying to get from Seattle to Vancouver, B.C., Canada try Express Shuttle. It's runs $24 from the Travelodge near the Space Needle to the Delta Resort in Vancouver. From there, it's a $3 ride to get to the airport.

PART TWO - TRAINS

Amtrak is the only commercial passenger line in the country. When they have rates comparable to the bus or airlines, it's the best mode of transportation. The seats are comfortable, the views are scenic and you can make all sorts of pals in the lounge.

THE BEST REASON OF ALL

Why do I love the train? I'll tell you. They have the best restrooms in the travel industry. They're big and there's plenty of them. You can actually attend your morning ritual in nice surroundings without having a line of people at your door. Plus, many of the stations have a wonderful aesthetic that is seriously lacking in bus stations and airports.

SETTLING IN

Make sure you have some reading material (see p. 87) or a Gameboy or crossword puzzles or something to keep you entertained. You have this huge lovely space to yourself. Stretch out, take a nap, get silently drunk, fall asleep reading the latest Henry Rollins book. For a diversion you can go to the viewing car, which still functioned (last time I checked) as the final outpost of smokerdom. Or you can go to the lounge and engage folks in conversation, a game of cards, or even dominoes (don't forget to bring the set). I wish the trains would start carrying board games. My pal Jen never travels without her portable magnetic backgammon set. Hell, if there's no one around to play with, she plays against herself.

TRAIN FOOD

The drinks are airline prices, but it's better than the bus which doesn't allow you to drink at all. The thing to do is take your own flask and mixers. If you don't drink, take your own beverages anyway. It'll still save you money in the long run. The train charges $1.25 for a can of pop. Now tell me, how ridiculous is that? But I'm not finger pointing, all means of travel reams passengers on sugar water.

Many Amtrak trains have dining cars and it's an elegant way to dine. The best meal? The sunshiny panoramic view is gorgeous and makes the oatmeal taste better. It's a less expensive menu than lunch or dinner but more filling. Lunch is a $6 sandwich, and dinner will be an $11 half-chicken. Stick with the breakfast for under $5.

AT NIGHT

If you have the dough, treat yourself to a sleeper. I don't know what they look like inside, I've never done it.

In coach, the temperature drops at night. I think it's to decrease the spread of germs. So remember to take your own blanket. This is very important otherwise you will be shelling out $12 for an Amtrak blanket. And while they are very nice blankets, $12 is a bit steep for what you're getting.

WORD TO THE WISE

Make sure you know your train schedule. I once got stranded in the Los Angeles train station because I got confused about the schedule. So, instead of a 2-hour layover, I had a 26-hour layover. I had too much luggage because I broke the Big Rule and only $12 in my pocket to last two days. It was relatively pleasant. I had stationery to write letters to friends and markers to draw and a copy of Atlas Shrugged.

In the morning, when the rush hour commuters where disembarking their trains, they caught full view of me in my sleeping bag, sleeping sitting up in those infernally uncomfortable station chairs.

"Oh, look," they said to each other, pointing at me. "Remember those days?" Then they laughed nostalgically and went on their way.

SNEAKING THE TRAIN

You can sneak on board the Amtrak train, I'm not going to tell you how (one way is to hide in the bathroom) but I will tell you, that if you're caught, tell the truth. Don't play the conductor for a fool, it insults their intelligence. Don't get belligerent or surly. Be polite, honest and calm. At least that's what a conductor pal told me. It some cases you'll be dropped off at the next stop, in worst case scenarios, you'll be handcuffed and handed over to the local sheriff.

PART THREE - PLANES

The best prices for airlines is if you get a 14-day or 21-day advance. But it makes changing those tickets harder because the airline considers those 'discounted' tickets. Call discount travel agencies and be very aware of the limitations of your ticket so that it doesn't end up costing you more down the line.

HOW TO PAY

Pay cash. If you put it on your credit card or a friend's credit card, remember that you'll be paying bizarrely high interest on that, if you don't pay the bill by the end of the month. The nice thing about plastic, though, is that instant gratification that it inspires. Use your judgment.

BE AWARE OF LIMITATIONS

The airline policies will bite you in the ass if you aren't wary and sometimes the friendly skies ain't so friendly. Let's say you bought a ticket on a 7-day advance and you want to extend your stay one or two more days? Sometimes the airlines will attempt to charge you the difference of the 7-day advance and a ticket purchased without advance at all. They consider it buying a new ticket. It's seems a little ridiculous, especially when you know that they have the seating available, that they're just being cheap and infernal.

There are ways around it. Airlines reward their loyal customers with frequent flyers passes and all sorts of cool perks. Having a frequent flyer card can mean big points and preferential treatment in the game of musical chairs. Also, initiate a relationship with a travel agency. They have their special interests as well, don't think their job is to book you on the best possible flight; it's to fill the seats in the airlines and certain airlines have priority over others.

OLD STANDBY TRICK

If you have the time to kill, use the old standby trick. If the airline has oversold the flight, they sometimes seek out volunteers to wait for the next one. The airline will often give you a free roundtrip ticket for doing them this favor, and a friend of mine even got $400. Oversold flights are more common than you might think, especially during the holidays.

GETTING TO THE AIRPORT

Most airports are located at the city's limits so getting out there with all your luggage can be a little problematic. Of course the best way is to have a pal with a car drop you off. But it doesn't always work that way.

Factor in $15-25 to and from the airport because that's how much a shuttle service costs. I like it because it delivers you to your door. Save a couple of dollars by checking the local Yellow Pages for shuttle ad specials listed under 'Airport Transportation'.

If there are more than two pals traveling together, splitting a taxi might be more affordable than you think. However, if you don't have the money, public transportation is cheap and reliable. There is almost always a bus or a train from the airport into town. It just takes a lot longer, but you'll get there. It's cost efficient but a huge pain in the ass if you have too much stuff.

CARTS

If you have a lot of baggage, keep your eyes peeled for abandoned carts by the gates as you're disembarking from the plane. Otherwise you will have to shell out $1.50 for a cart near the baggage services, and I think that's a rip-off. The airport in Vancouver BC has free carts available, why do American airports have to be so damn cheap and money grubby?

AIRPORT FOOD

Don't look at it, don't eat it. It's not real and it's probably not very good. I know, I know, it looks good but it'll only cause you pain in the end. I will give you permission to get a frozen yogurt, that won't mess you up inside. Also, don't even think of having a drink there. The airports are notorious for ripping people off. That's because they think that people who travel are people who have money to burn. That old expense account mentality, but it doesn't wash here.

PART FOUR - DRIVEAWAY CARS

What a deal. There are people who move from one part of the country to somewhere else, and they need someone to drive their car for them. So they hire a company who lets you drive their car. You pay for gas, food, and lodging but otherwise have a free ride with a few limitations. Here's how it works:

Look in the daily newspaper's classified ads under 'Transportation' or in the Yellow Pages under 'Automobile Transporters and Drive-Away Companies'. Call them up and tell them where you want to go and when. Be flexible. If you want to go to New York, be willing to end up in New Jersey or Connecticut (you can jump on a bus or train to New York from there). Be flexible with your departure date within a week of what you had in mind.

Go to the company's office and fill out an application. Have your valid driver's license with you as well as the names, addresses, and phone numbers of three references. Give your references a heads-up that they may get a call from the company. A $300 cash deposit is required, and it will be refunded to you when the car is delivered to its destination.

The company limits the number of days and miles you can drive the car, so don't expect a leisurely months-long tour of the States and Canada. About 10 days is the typical limitation on a coast-to-coast expedition but that's actually plenty of time for exploration, relaxation and fun. Minimum driver's age for most companies is 21, and the car owners are responsible for the car if it breaks down, and the owners' insurance covers you in case of an accident.

It's a crapshoot what kind of car you'll get, but the last time Jen did a driveaway she got a new car that operated on diesel fuel, and it only used up a half tank between New York City and Pittsburgh, Pennsylvania, which is pretty amazing. That car was a lot nicer than the 20-year-old beaters she was used to driving, that's for sure.

If you're not in a hurry, like to drive, and have a traveling buddy, this is one of the cheapest and most fun ways to go.

NOMAD TIP

Hit the Ground Running

With any mode of transportation, it's best if you schedule your arrival during the daytime instead of at night. It's safer that way, and it's easier to find a ride. Taxis and shuttles are easier then and public transportation is more available. Plus traveling at night ensures that you'll get some sleep and you'll be ready to hit the ground on your arrival. A shot of Nyquil in the restroom before boarding the plane can do wonders for your sinuses and ability to sleep soundly. If the flight is less than 3 hours, skip the Nyquil and take an Advil instead.

I'M UNEMPLOYED AND I LIKE IT.

EMPLOYMENT ENDEAVORS

FINDING A JOB

You just landed in town, the first priority (assuming you don't have that elusive nest egg) is to get a job. Usually I'll go to the neighborhood bar and strike up a conversation with the bartender. If anyone knows where jobs are, they do. Also, if you want to make your grand debut into the scene, the best place to look for a job is at the local alternative paper. Having some skills help, but a willingness to do just about anything takes you a little farther.

Walk around the neighborhood you're staying in, a lot of local shops will put a sign in the window if they're looking for help. Also, try a temp agency. Besides office help, they'll employ people for light physical labor, too. So you might find yourself in an aromatherapy assembly line or you might find yourself doing the catch-up filing for a paint store. They ask that you make yourself presentable (tuck in a clean shirt) and take punctuality seriously. Reasonable enough request, and in exchange you get a flexible schedule and a steady paycheck.

If you need money immediately, you might try being a day laborer where you get paid cash at the end of the day. If you can wait, two weeks will be the turnover time to get your first temp paycheck and weekly after that.

If you're looking for something more stable, have no fear, many of these temp jobs morph into permanent positions.

INTERNSHIPS

You can get a great job by becoming an intern, the only thing is that the pay isn't so great. But you're in an environment where you get to learn skills in your field of interest. The thing about internships is that they will turn into jobs, so investigate what you want to do and remember that nearly every major company has an internship program.

ALTERNATIVE WAYS OF MAKING MONEY

Garage Sales

Clean out your cupboards, then put the stuff on the sidewalk on Saturday morning. Make a few signs near the big streets so you get traffic and take any reasonable offer. If you're really organized, do this with a few friends. That way you'll have more junk to sell and more fun with pals.

Flea Markets

If you are artsy crafty in any way, then load it up and take it to the flea market. The booth space runs about $25 per day, but take a thermos and a table, settle in and have fun meeting people. A lot of people will take their garage sale there, because you get a ton of foot traffic and high percentage on actually unloading all the stuff.

Selling Your Plasma

This is a quick fix when you're at the bottom of the barrel and 412 can make all the difference. Some people actually depend on plasma sales on a regular basis, but they have alcohol habits they're trying to support. You will not be accepted if you have acquired any tattoos in the past year. If you're HIV positive, a needle user or a high risk for AIDS, don't even consider it, you could kill someone with your blood.

Selling Your CDs. Clothes and Books

The stores that buy this stuff are not necessarily interested in giving you a good deal on the stuff you bring in to sell. My friends have better luck putting a blanket on Haight Street and sidewalk vending. But if you need a few bucks fast, swallow the burning pain and take a box of stuff for the clerk to sort through.

Bake Sale

Like to bake? Make a bunch of cookies, brownies

or snacks, wrap individual servings in plastic and hawk them at the park or concerts. Ask for $1 donation or trade. You'll be surprised what kind of offers you get.

Busking

If you are a decent musician and entertaining as a person, consider street playing to make some income. If you know a lot of popular songs, especially the folksy Sixties stuff, people will find some change for you. I have seen tap dancers and brass bands do this during the holiday season, and it not only attracts a crowd but provides some revenue.

Panhandling

This is straight up asking strangers for cash. I think it's tacky, but there have been times where I've been tempted but my mother didn't raise a beggar. A friend of mine says he pulls in $10-$15 a day, which is pretty good considering he doesn't have to pay any rent or bills.

Laboratory Experiment

In any town that has a student hospital, there will be tests and experiments that they'll pay you to be a part of. The prospect of becoming a human guinea pig doesn't appeal, but some people find it helpful and, not to mention, quite lucrative.

TOP 10 JOBS
Easy to Get... Easy to Quit

waitress/waiter
dishwasher
janitor/cleaning lady
flower vendor
coffee slinger
security guard
anything retail
phone sex worker
typist/data entry
file clerk

MAGGIE?! AIN'T YA SUPPOSED TO BE WORKIN' RIGHT NOW?
I QUIT YESTERDAY, DANITA. NONE OF THAT SPINNIN' SHAKES SHIT FOR ME NO MORE.

IN THE SHADOW OF JOE: MY LIFE AS A ROADIE

BUCKY SINISTER

"Don't let Darren jump out of moving vehicles," Mike informed me. I had asked him what the most important thing about my job was as a roadie for his band, Steel Pole Bath Tub. My guess would've been driving, selling t-shirts, or something that had to do with the actual job description, but, as I discovered in the following 30 days, being a roadie had a lot to do with managing the sometimes strange personal habits of the band members, and dealing with unusual circumstances that popped up like weeds after a rain.

My roadie job was the best roadtrip I've ever experienced, and the most fun I've ever had for a month straight. I got to see the country from Portland, Oregon, to Portland, Maine while seeing my favorite band play more than 20 times. On top of all that, I got paid. That's right, kids, I actually made more money traveling with the band schlepping gear than I was making at my job back home selling books. I think it's great work, but there are only so many bands out there and almost all of them already have roadies. Getting a roadie job is like many other jobs: you can't be one until you've been one. I lucked into my lone roadie gig by being a friend of the band.

Their regular roadie was a guy named Joe. Joe could drive any vehicle no matter how long, with any size U-Haul trailer on the back, for 36 hours straight on a diet of chewing gum and Vivarin. He could parallel park while stringing a guitar. Joe could do whatever was needed, on a moment's notice, to perfection. I heard all about this every time I fell short of his legend. The farther along the tour got, the mightier the feats of Joe: the time Joe killed a polar bear outside Kodiak, Alaska with a mikestand; Joe's secret method of making espresso involving a strange contraption hooked up to the radiator that he had fashioned himself; and how he adjusted the timing belt of the van while it was still moving, strapping himself to the bottom of the van Indiana Jones style, so the band wouldn't be late for soundcheck. There was no way that I could've outperformed Joe, but here are some tips and ideas that I picked up along the way.

Keep the fanboys away. The ironic point to this one is that I was a fanboy myself. Most of the time they are too intimidated to actually to talk to the band anyway, so chatting it up with the roadie for inside dirt on the band is as close as they want to come. Some, however, believe themselves to be bonafide friends of the band. The deluded ones often have a sense of bad timing about their interactions, as well. Joe was actively recruited by the Secret Service and the FBI for their Witness Relocation Program.

Provide the band with their drinks of choice. It's extremely important to snag drinks for the band. I saw quite a few bars that absolutely would not serve after a certain time whether you are with the band or are the band. These times were always while the band was in the middle of a set. There was no time and no way of asking them what they wanted to drink. Don't be embarrassed to order two double bourbons, two Scotch and waters, and four beers at last call. C'mon, this is rock and roll, baby! Other bands may have other appetites... you may be called upon to go score, buy, or whatnot. In dire times, Joe had a method of fermenting Gatorade and making margaritas out of it.

Stay awake with the host. Until bands get really huge, they often stay at people's houses. These people are usually party types, willing to invite a strange rock band into their house. These people do not sleep. Somehow, cheap beer keeps them awake. They are often oracles of All Ideas Cockamamie, and you are a fresh ear. Your job is to stay awake with those people as they blabber about their theories on which lousy band is better, Cheap Trick or Kiss, while the band sleeps on. Joe could sleep, nod, and say, "Uh-huh, I see your point," all at the same time.

Keep track of the band members. We only lost Darren twice, once in Seattle and once in New York. Crafty little devil, he is. He jumped out of the van in New York. My vindication was that day in New York, I was chillin back at the hotel when he flipped out and split. Timing is everything when you're on the road, and not being able to find one person is maddening. While finding Darren in record time in Detroit one tour, Joe found Jimmy Hoffa first.

Don't puke in the van. I consumed at least one pint of hard liquor a day. That's my safe estimate, I can't really say for sure. It was kind of a steady, slow burn through an alcoholic haze. At all the stops where the band sold out the club, the grateful owners just kept pouring me one after another. Hey, it's okay to get completely blotto, but it's practically impossible to get vomit smells out of a Ford Econoline. We spent at least eight hours a day on average in that van, and it's bad enough having to smell each other, much less having to smell recycled Old Crow. Joe could rip off his shirt and make a barf bag out of it in 3.2 seconds.

Being a roadie for just a month spoiled me for normal living upon my return. I had to pay to see bands. I had to pay for drinks. I had to leave bars at two in the morning. I was expected not to have hangovers at work. I had to look at the same people every day. Perhaps the best aspect of being a roadie was that the experience left me with at least 30 stories, and it's always great telling stories to people I don't know that well when I can introduce them with, "Once, when I was a roadie..."

©Jaime Hernandez

©Keith Knight

HANGING OUT

PUBLIC TRANSPORTATION

I love public transportation, especially in a city that means it. Not having a car means not having to worry about parking, insurance, registration and security. Some cities have terrible public transportation. Research your destination before you make any decisions whether to take the car or not. Cabs are an affordable luxury, especially when there's more than one person to split the ride. Bus passes are the best deal if that's your primary mode of transport, otherwise the bus runs $1 a ride on average. Also invest in a bus schedule and map, it costs $3 but it tells you where you're going and about how long it's going to take to get there.

TAKING CARE OF YOUR HEALTH

There are free clinics and doctors who charge on a sliding scale basis. Don't let poverty send you from taking care of your health. You won't be denied medical care if it's urgent, and if it's not urgent, the clinic will fit you into their schedule. Sometimes the doctor will give you samples of medication instead of a prescription that you have to pay for. Also, consider alternative medicine like massage therapy and aromatherapy. These are affordable and positive approaches to maintaining your health.

If you're a woman, don't forget to get a pap smear every year. The local Planned Parenthood is a place I recommend calling, because they can take care of your birth control as well. They can also refer you where to get affordable AIDS testing and support services.

Tooth problems can cause excruciating pain. Many cities have a school of professional dentistry, which provides a low-cost or free way to get your teeth cleaned or fixed. Look in the phone book, call them up and ask if the students need patients to work on. They almost always do.

RENTING A ROOM

Residential Hotels

No deposit required, but the weekly costs add up. It may be cheaper to rent a room in a group apartment or house if you have the money.

Food Co-op/Grocery Store Kiosks

This is the best place to check about housing.

There is invariably a bulletin board full of people looking to sublet, rent, and/or share housing. Check there first.

Roommate Referral Services

Very intense way to look for housing. You pay a flat fee and proceed to call every available room listed within your budget. On the other side, the house looking for a new roomy has to interview literally dozens of folks until they cull their selection. It wears thin for everyone involved, but I know people who have had a great experience this way.

Hostels

Very reasonable rates for shared living situations. I think they discourage extended stays but as a landing point, highly recommended.

Word of Mouth

My favorite way to find out about anything. Let people around you know you're looking for a place and usually someone will know someone who is looking for a roommate.

GETTING WHAT YOU PAY FOR

I have never paid more than $400 for a room in any city I've lived. The living situation has ranged from great to shitty (current situation being great, the crank house situation being shitty). I don't have much stuff or much money, and that yearning to explore other cities has made it hard to lay down any roots. Like many other people, my family's home is my permanent address.

It's easier for me and the way I live to join a house, as opposed to establishing a house. I don't have access to much cash, and I'm not sure how I feel about being responsible for a household of people (especially after watching some pals get burned from delinquent roommates). It takes a lot of trust, otherwise you might find yourself paying other people's bills.

If there are heavy politics involved and personality conflicts are flaring up, try to find an omnibudsman, otherwise there's no resolution and everyone will walk away from the experience feeling profoundly burned.

MAINTAINING PEACE

Try to be cordial with your roommates. Be willing to share the commonalities of the kitchen, such as the milk, bread, juice. If you find your cookie stash constantly broken into, keep your goodies in your room. Try to keep the living areas clean, wash up after yourself when cooking. There's nothing worse than waking up the next morning to a sinkful of dirty dishes that don't belong to you. Don't be a rigid jerk about it; it isn't worth blowing a gasket over a cup and a bowl. If one of your roommates requests some quiet time, don't respond by blasting your music through the walls. Consideration is important. If you both indulge, share your vices. If the sharing is one-sided, then stop being so generous. If you don't mind, then by all means go ahead.

WASHING DISHES

Some houses have a rotating schedule, others have a dishwasher. Some houses' duties are split between the cooking and the cleaning. Our house, full of bachelors, depends on cleaning your own mess up after yourself. Of course, there is some crossover and no one is too uptight about a few dirty dishes. I have lived in places where we played the waiting game - seeing how long it would take for the others to break down and do the whole mess of dishes. I have lost. I have lived with some hardcore slobs.

WHEN IN ROME

When you live with slobs, give in to their slob ways or else you will be the housecleaner for the whole motley Brady Bunch. This is the perfect opportunity to invite a needy pal to sofasurf with you; you can make him or her the maid for a couple of months or so. If you live in an ultra-neat house, try to keep up as best you can. More than likely, however, you're living with an obsessive-compulsive and he or she will have total control over the cleanliness of the house (in other words, your cleaning job will never be good enough).

Do not leave food in your room. It creates a terrible smell that permeates the house, none of your roommates will want to look for it, and the rats and cockroaches will congregate there. No, seriously, don't let your room become a haven for all the glasses and coffee cups in the house.

ESTABLISHING RULES

If Your Name Is On The Lease

Find out how much money the prospective roommates have, how they intend to get money, what their relationship is with their families, the extent of their drug use, the kind of work they like to do. In other words, find out if they have a life. People in need of housing will say anything to find a place. Ask about their taste in music, if they have a girlfriend or boyfriend, their political point-of-view. Ask yourself honestly, "Can I deal with this person before coffee every morning?"

If You're Getting A Room In The House

Find out how much you owe every month. Pay it. Discuss with other roommates the expectations about the living situation. Hopefully you will agree. At least, agree to compromise.

WHEN ARE YOU GETTING OUT OF MY LIFE?

Sometimes it's really hard to get rid of that special person. I've known lease holders who have resorted to eviction notices, I have seen people run up backrent over the $1,000 mark. There has to be that happy medium, otherwise your home could be a battlefield. The best way to get rid of someone is to find them a better gig. Hope that they honor the house debts, or if you're just happy to see them go, write off the losses as a lesson learned. Don't accept their collect calls.

LIVING IN A DANGEROUS NEIGHBORHOOD

Take it from personal experience. Do not live near railroad tracks, the downtown bus station, the plasma center or a mortuary. These are not only weird energy hangouts for transient natures but it also lends to large open spaces of asphalt, not enough residences around.

I lived in a space that had an 8-foot chainlink fence wrapped with razor wire at the top. By the time I left, my car had been broken into more times than I care to remember (lucky I didn't have a gun!), the side entrance door was mangled so badly, if I had stayed an evening more who's telling what could have happened (I'll give you a hint, it wouldn't have been good).

I mean, I lived in a deserted alley between El Madrid bar and the Salazar mortuary, every night you could hear gunfire impressing even old school punk bands visiting from Los Angeles. The roach infestation made it much worse.

What kind of hell did I deserve to live there? It was a terrible combination of an impulse decision and desperation. What was I thinking? I was thinking that I was going to move into a cool art space with some friends, and got the short and very dangerous end of a no-bathroom deal.

If you have to live in these types of neighborhoods, make sure you have at least one male roommate. Don't let the house schedule get too predictable, some thieves will case the house for weeks to establish the pattern. (You kind of wish they would rob people who actually had something, but it's the same mentality that drives people to burn down their own neighborhoods.)

The best way to live in one of these neighborhoods is in a commune of nihilist/artists where everything is run down, the parties are the loudest on the block, the rents are cheap and visitors passed-out in the front yard on Saturday mornings are a common occurrence. It makes neighbors say, "Man, those people are fucked up," and you'll be left alone.

TIPS TO AVOID BEING RIPPED OFF

• Keep your car clean.
• If the neighborhood is really bad, either park your car in the garage or keep the doors unlocked so you don't have to keep replacing windows
• Buy a pull-out stereo, or reduce your musical listening pleasure to a cheap boombox.
• Buy a steering wheel lock. (The steering wheel can often be sawed apart to get it off, but it makes a good first-level visual deterrent. If a thief has a choice between a car with a steering wheel lock and one without, he'll go for the one without every time.)
• Keep the doors in your house locked.
• Don't let strangers in the house (especially when you're alone).
• Know your neighbors, exchange phone numbers with them.
• Join the NRA and plaster the stickers on your car and home.

LIVING WITH PEOPLE YOU HATE

Don't do this. Usually it takes less than a month to determine that this living situation isn't going to work out. If you have the lease, try to break the news gently. Usually, people can agree on a separation date. If your words fall on deaf ears, serve an eviction notice. This gives them a finite period of time with which to get their stuff out of there. Of course, if they know they system, they also know that they can tie this up in court for an extra month or two. Is this how you want to live with someone that you hate?

If neither of you hold the lease, the best thing you can do is not give too much quarter and cross your fingers that he or she doesn't fuck your friends. If he or she becomes part of the family that way, uncross your fingers and put a pot of tea on the stove to boil. Once that happens, he's practically a lifer, no matter how far back he falls in rent. Stay in your room. Read books. You'll get used to it, believe me.

The third alternative to this, of course, is to move out yourself. If you can find a place to stay, and you don't have too much stuff, this is definitely something to think about. I mean, I only recommend this when things are really bad. This is where the whole house is collapsing from the inside, there are alcoholic loser musicians sleeping on the kitchen floor, the hostility level is rising in direct proportion to the amount of crank in the house, all the food is being consumed by human parasites and psychosis abounds. (I was reluctant to leave this last place as I had just painted my bedroom.)

STAYING POWER

If you like where you live and the people you live with, try to establish some staying power. Opt to sublet your space instead of giving it up. Make arrangements while you're gone to cover your expenses. Try taking on some of the household responsibilities outside of the general chores, like the phone or the electric.

If you first move into a house, please don't trying to establish staying power by advocating a bunch of changes. Don't throw out the couch or replace the curtains or talk about painting. It's insulting to the people that live there and such changes are gradual and these suggestions usually come out of the mouths of flakes.

NASTY HABITS

You will find that some people that you live with have some very nasty habits. Taxidermy can be one of those strange habits (and the smell!) unless you're into that sort of thing. Others have an obsession with pornography. I say, who cares, as long as they're not jacking off in the living room when you're walking in the door.

Other nasty habits include that player habit of bringing over a different lay all the time. You keep running into a new half-naked stranger each morning which is only interesting for a little while (tell your pal to get his or her own place; too much traffic). The flipside of that is the regular boyfriend or girlfriend that suddenly takes up residence in your home. How annoying! I understand lovers want to be together all the time, but it gets a little much. Move in together, why don't you, but not over here.

You know what used to really get to me? When people didn't rinse out the shower and I had to clean up their sludge and pick their hair out of the drain. I thought that was sick. And people who left their cigarettes smoldering in their rooms. I've had pals who've been burned out of their homes. I would hate that.

TELEPHONE: The Deal With The Devil

We don't have long distance in the house anymore. No one could take responsibility for their calls, and the house ate a big chunk of past roommates' debts. It's highly annoying sometimes, but I see the rationale and reluctantly agree. If you are in charge of the phone, give copies of the long distance bill to all the roommates along with the estimated total. Try to keep on top of your phone bill, and keep a phone log so you know which phone calls are yours when the inevitable argument comes around.

FORWARDING MAIL

There's a form you can get from the post office to forward your mail when you leave. Also, leave your new address and phone number near the phone, so the information can be forwarded to interested parties.

If you leave on a bad note, like leaving a bunch of debt or ill sentiments, don't expect too much from the roommates. Keep in mind that most roommates are flakes. Don't expect too much anyway.

SHARING A ROOM

If you travel as much as I do, you might try this. I ended up sharing a 7x12 room with a friend of a friend. There was a loft built in so we had a stacked bunkbed style living arrangement. I tell you, it was a good thing I traveled so much; even though I was paying next to nothing in rent, our styles got exceedingly cramped after about a year. Basically I came off the road, and wanted some changes around these parts. It all worked out for the best, she found her way to the Big Apple and last I heard, she's sharing space with another former roommate.

If you decide to share a room, avoid having a steady boyfriend or girlfriend. No one likes to be in the other bed while you're trying to get it on. It's extremely tacky, actually, unless you're pervy that way. Mostly, though, it's inconsiderate. (And don't do it in the other bed without washing the linen afterwards. That's just plain gross.)

SIGNING A LEASE

Signing a lease? If you're by yourself, make sure either you have good credit or a wad of cash and connections. Be prepared to pay first and last months' rent and a deposit. Knowing someone credible in the building who can vouch for you to the landlord can make a big difference, especially if you're new in town and/or marginally employed. Your friends and future landlords will only take a chance on you if you are reliable. You can only burn people once, then you aren't ever welcome back again.

If you're getting a room in a house with one person on the lease, try to see a copy of the lease so that you are not being jacked with more than your share of the rent.

OPENING A BANK ACCOUNT

Play nice with the banks. Even you if owe them two dollars, they'll send it to some major information database for banks and financial institutions across the country and you're locked out from ever opening another bank account for seven years. It's quite ridiculous. They'll spend more money being assholes and ruining your name, than resolving it without it going on that dreaded permanent record. If you are truly locked out, never fear, in major metropolitan cities there is usually a bank or two around that will accept bad risks like you; at a price, of course.

The other alternative is going to one of those neighborhood check-cashing places. These are truly the poor man's bank. They ream you with high fees and act like they're doing you a favor. And maybe they are. After all, what is the alternative? There are not that many jobs that pay cash under the table. Whatever you do, avoid taking a loan with them. They're worse than the devil, and if you're a procrastinator, they like you so much the better. That just drives up the service charges.

I ALREADY TOLD YOU THAT MY ROOMMATES WOULD HAVE A FIT IF I LET YOU STAY WITH US! WE ALREADY HAVE FIVE PEOPLE LIVING IN A 4-ROOM APARTMENT!...
OKAY! OKAY! I THOUGHT YOU WERE MY FRIEND, GUESS I WAS WRONG!

SLACK ATTACK
WAMMO

I've got a place now. Well, sort of. It's a no water, one room rehearsal space in a building chocked full of band gear and assorted musician scum just like me. To me it's a fucking paradise. $118 a month, all bills paid. The only trick is showering but I've got that covered all over town. When I got my first shitty little record advance, I was able to buy Timbuk 3's old '86 Plymouth Voyager. It's beat to hell and burns oil like a smoking hookah but it gets me around town. Barbara sold it to me cheap. Hell, we were both delighted that my demo landed me a deal, no matter how small. So now I've got a record out and a place to sleep. My other band, the Asylum Street Spankers, is doing pretty well. Well enough to keep me fed, clothed, and knee deep in beer, wine, whiskey, and cigars. It's funny, if you're in a popular band in this town, the world is your oyster.

The free beer flows, no cover at any bar, you sit down at a restaurant and the free appetizer or bottle of wine appears at your table. It's as if I pulled a cornucopia of sex and slack right out of my ass. Discounts at the music stores. Shit, Dale at Workhorse Guitars gave me a couple of small amps for free just because I put him on my record. The Spankers have all quit their dayjobs. When we tour, we stay in hotels. That's a far cry from any other band I've been in. Christ, when I think of the places I've crashed all over the country, it still doesn't measure up to my 12-year squat in Austin. Oh, it's been an on/again-off/again thing but much more on than off. Even now I still don't have a shower. But that's my own choice, really.

It all started back in January of 1986. I was working as a DJ in this crappy hotel disco. My old band, Oboyo, was playing a kind of punkfunkskathrash mix. Kinda like the shit I hear on the radio now. (God, I'm starting to sound like one of those "I started it all and everyone ripped off my ideas" assholes.) I quit or got fired from a string of club DJ jobs and kept getting hired for more money elsewhere. If you're a musician, getting told what to play as a DJ can really put the bite on your soul. I went through a bad love affair and broke my hand punching a refrigerator. I started hitting the bottle pretty hard, mixing booze with whatever drugs were around. The band broke up and I went into some serious depression. I got trashed every night, ready to fight or fuck. I did a lot of both. I had been living at a co-op as an unofficial member but I became such an obnoxious idiot, they threw me out. I started seriously couch surfing then, crashing everywhere. Staying all night at parties and passing out. Sleeping at punk rock houses. I had all my shit stashed at friends' houses and I would just move my stuff from one person's garage to the next. The hardest night I ever spent was when I slept on the street in the dead of winter. I've never known such bitter chilling misery and my heart goes out to anyone who has to face that kind of hardship.

It took me a while to figure out how to successfully survive without a home and without losing all your friends. It's not easy. Some of you would be better off just abiding by the rules and playing the straight and narrow. I couldn't go that route. Sometimes I wonder if I was ever meant to have a real place at all.

Every time I've rented a house or an apartment, it's ended in disaster. I once ended a long homeless streak by moving into a house full of artists. I was in a band called Minus Grace at the time and things were going pretty well. We left for a month-long tour of the East Coast. Three of us and all our gear in a '69 Malibu. The guitar player was a friend of Michael Stipe's and we crashed on his floor in Athens. The next day he came up and put his arm around my shoulders. He told me a mutual friend of ours had called him and I'd better call home. Sure enough, the house I had just moved into had burned to the ground. After the tour, I left Austin immediately to go on the road with Poi Dog Pondering. I couchsurfed in San Francisco toward the end of that tour and got back to Austin after about two months.

I held down a few shitty jobs here and there and never really got a place to live until I began deejaying at the infamous Cannibal Club. That's probably the cushiest job I've ever had. I spun whatever records I wanted to, slacked off while the bands were playing, free drinks, drugs, sex... the ne'er-do-well's paradise, no? You'd think so but I got burned out anyway. I decided in 1991 after getting fired from a radio station for playing Ice T's *Freedom of Speech*, I would survive off of my art and avoid straight jobs like the plague.

It was a long haul. I broke down once and drove a cab for a couple months. Now I play music, write poetry and songs, paint, do performance art, compete in poetry slams, and act. Here's a little tidbit - I played the only person in the movie *Slacker* who talks about his job. Ironic, eh?

Okay, here are a few guidelines to successful couch surfing but I'm not gonna give up all my tricks. Sure, things are going swell for me right now but the pendulum always swings back to smack you in the ass. And I'll be damned if I'm gonna sleep outside because your ass is already on the couch.

Wammo's Mighty Couch Surfing Tips

ALWAYS behave in a manner that will get you invited back. Be polite, courteous, observe the rules of the house. If you have food, contraband, booze, whatever, share them. If your host does not want to partake, go elsewhere to get wasted, unless you are absolutely fucking sure that your host doesn't care if you party in their home. If they let you, don't make a habit of it. If you are staying with someone you're having sex with, be the best lover possible. Fuck the mattress off of the bed and the posters from the walls. Shake the ceiling and make the neighbors' dogs howl. Try things you've never even thought of before and listen to the needs of your partner. (You should be doing all of this anyway.) However, if you are fucking someone just so you can have a place to crash, get out. You are only hurting them and yourself. Tragedy awaits.

DON'T rip anyone off. There is a huge difference between slacking and scamming. If you steal from someone, not only have you fucked yourself in their eyes but you will quickly develop a reputation as a hustler who won't be welcome anywhere.

DON'T stay in one place too long. The last thing anyone wants is a guest who will never leave. Keep many options for places to stay open and use them wisely.

TRY to get back on your feet. I know dealing with the responsibilities of modern society sucks. But you've got to figure something out. Otherwise you'll find yourself bumming spare change and drinking MD2020 at the age of 45. Do something, start a band, paint, draw sidewalk art, write fucking poetry, get a job as a critic. By the way, you can usually find someone at poetry readings who will let you crash at their place for a few days.

HOUSESIT. If you're in it for the long haul, this is a cherry way to achieve total slack. People are always leaving town. Vacations, tours, business trips, whatever, be a reliable housesitter and you're home free, if you'll pardon the pun. Just remember these rules: Always have the house spotless when they return home. Make sure you get their permission to entertain in their house and keep your guests down to one or two at a time. Don't throw any parties. Don't kill any pets or plants. If you do this occasionally you could probably obtain enough references to start your own housesitting business. Then you could get paid for fucking off. Ah, the ultimate slack dream.

AVOID other deadbeats. I'm a deadbeat. You're a deadbeat. We're all deadbeats. Wouldn't you like to be a deadbeat, too? The last thing you want to do is let someone else who doesn't have a place to crash know that you've found a good squat. I guarantee you that they will show up and they will never leave. Believe me, I've seen it happen again and again. If you're squatting in an empty or abandoned space, they'll move in and invite their own friends to stay. If you try to throw them out, you'll get the old "You don't pay rent here" retort. The more people that come and go from a place, the more attention it will attract. Pretty soon things will get out of hand and the cops will show up. Then it's back on the street. If you are crashing on someone's couch, staying at a co-op or any other situation where you are depending on the generosity of an individual or committee, informing other deadbeats will fuck up your situation quicker than you can say "skid row."

Alrighty then, you kids be careful out there and try

to play nice. Stay warm and dry. Bathe often. Keep your teeth clean. Avoid dark alleys and intravenous drugs. When it comes to sex, play safe. Good luck and God bless.

* HUFF *
* PUFF *
WHERE AM I?

EPILOGUE

Sofasurfing is not only a lifestyle but an art form. If it's done right, you can do your small part to spread happiness and goodwill throughout your corner of the universe. Done badly, a houseguest can be an agent of disease and pestilence. Sometimes it's just a matter of the host's interpretation.

Traveling is one of life's best ways to gain perspective on the world. Most of us can't afford it as tourists (and who would want to, anyway?) so we sleep on the sofas and floors of friends and the friends of friends that will let us.

You never know what's going to happen when you don't have a place to live. That's the tricky part, getting through it, keeping positive and not becoming a burden to your friends. Sometimes it can last the span of a short vacation, an exciting little romp to another city, or it can morph into a desperate long haul filled with unemployment and frustration.

Being a good houseguest can be the easiest thing in the world. Just try to keep to the simple guidelines, pack lightly, clean up after yourself, and above all, don't kill anything. The big key is, be considerate and don't overstay your welcome.

FURTHER READING

These are some books that may interest you further:

World Stompers by Brad Olsen
101 Things To Do Before the Revolution by Claire Wolfe
99-cents a Meal Cookbook by Ruth and Bill Kaysing
The Art & Science of Dumpster Diving by John Hoffman

BREATHING EXERCISE FOR RELAXATION

Breathe in deeply
Breathe in deeply to the count of four
Hold it to the count of four
Expel through the mouth to the count of eight
Breathe in
Breathe out
Breathe in
Breathe out
Repeat

©Eve Gilbert

MANIC D PRESS BOOKS

Growing Up Free In America. *Bruce Jackson.* $11.95

Devil Babe's Big Book of Fun! *Isabel Samaras.* $11.95

Dances With Sheep. *Keith Knight.* $11.95

Monkey Girl. *Beth Lisick.* $11.95

Bite Hard. *Justin Chin.* $11.95

Next Stop: Troubletown. *Lloyd Dangle.* $10.95

The Hashish Man and other stories. *Lord Dunsany.* $11.95

Forty Ouncer. *Kurt Zapata.* $11.95

The Unsinkable Bambi Lake. *Bambi Lake with Alvin Orloff.* $11.95

Hell Soup: the collected writings of Sparrow 13 LaughingWand. $8.95

Revival: spoken word from Lollapalooza 94. *edited by Juliette Torrez, Liz Belile, Mud Baron & Jennifer Joseph.* $12.95

The Ghastly Ones & Other Fiendish Frolics. *Richard Sala.* $9.95

The Underground Guide to San Francisco. *Jennifer Joseph, ed.* $10.95

King of the Roadkills. *Bucky Sinister.* $9.95

Alibi School. *Jeffrey McDaniel.* $8.95

Signs of Life: channel-surfing through '90s culture. *edited by Jennifer Joseph & Lisa Taplin.* $12.95

Beyond Definition: new writing from gay & lesbian san francisco *edited by Marci Blackman & Trebor Healey.* $10.95

Love Like Rage. *Wendy-o Matik* $7.00

The Language of Birds. *Kimi Sugioka* $7.00

The Rise and Fall of Third Leg. *Jon Longhi* $9.95

Specimen Tank. *Buzz Callaway* $10.95

The Verdict Is In. *edited by Kathi Georges & Jennifer Joseph* $9.95

Elegy for the Old Stud. *David West* $7.00

The Back of a Spoon. *Jack Hirschman* $7.00

Mobius Stripper. *Bana Witt* $8.95

Baroque Outhouse/Decapitated Head of a Dog. *Randolph Nae* $7.00

Graveyard Golf and other stories. *Vampyre Mike Kassel* $7.95

Bricks and Anchors. *Jon Longhi* $8.00

The Devil Won't Let Me In. *Alice Olds-Ellingson* $7.95

Greatest Hits. *edited by Jennifer Joseph* $7.00

Lizards Again. *David Jewell* $7.00

The Future Isn't What It Used To Be. *Jennifer Joseph* $7.00

Please add $2.50 to all orders for postage and handling.

Manic D Press
Box 410804
San Francisco CA 94141 USA

manicd@sirius.com http://www.sirius.com/~manicd/

Distributed to the Trade
in the US & Canada by Publishers Group West
in the UK & Europe by Turnaround Distribution